A Distant Friendly Party

Dick Brownson

Edward Gaskell
DEVON

First published 2013
Edward Gaskell publishers
Park Cottage
East-the-Water
Bideford
Devon
EX39 4AS

ISBN 978-1-906769-42-0

A Distant
Friendly
Party

Dick Brownson

Typeset, printed and bound by
Lazarus Press
Caddsdown Business Park
Bideford
Devon
EX39 3DX
www.lazaruspress.com

Edward Gaskell
publishers
DEVON

Cover Design and Graphics by
Nikki Brownson

Lazarus Press

By the same author

Wild Bill Longley
Texas Gunslinger

This book is dedicated to anyone who
ever pulled on a boxing glove and to
those who wish they had but never did
. . . and to a young Archie.

The days come and go like muffled and veiled figures
sent from a distant friendly party, but they say nothing,
and if we do not use the gifts they bring,
they carry them as silently away.

Ralph Waldo Emerson.

I read these lines above the door of a boxing gym well over half a century ago and they've stayed with me ever since. Talent and outstanding ability bestowed on youth in the sporting world and not taken advantage of is gradually 'carried away'. . . and then it's all too late.

My book is the story of a boxing gym over a pub in the nineteen fifties and the boxers who trained there, and of course the trainers, managers, promoters and the characters who hang around boxing. They were hard times, the like of which are not seen in this country today. . . or understood for that matter. Ten years after the end of the second world war, cities were still littered with bomb damage.

I'm often asked where are the photographs from that era, well, very few boxing people I knew could afford a camera. An occasional group photograph, or if you were a bit special, a single shot after adopting a fighting pose like John L. Sullivan!

I married the great niece of Dick and Bella Burge, who founded the Ring at Blackfriars in London. Dick fought for a World Title and also went to prison accused of fixing horse races but redeemed himself by outstanding service in the Great War.

He died in 1918, beloved and sadly missed by the sporting world. Bella lived to old age with an active life well into the nineteen fifties and could still out drink me: quite a feat in those days!

Since 1949, when I had my first amateur bout, I've never been far from boxing at all levels and seen many changes, not all for the 'good of the game.' It was a different world in those days and that is what this novel is all about.

Be prepared for some rough language and comments, but that's how it was and how I've told it.

Dick Brownson
Bideford, North Devon.

1

'**A** shithole! That's what this gym has become. And you know who said it? Fatal! And if he noticed, it's got to be right! Gloves, bandages, bloody rag, bits of paper all over the place and the locker doors are still hanging off! A pigsty! Probably how you all live at home; that is if any of you still *have* a home!'

This is Harry's weekly outburst usually when nursing a hangover. Harry Keys, a professional boxer before the war took his best years away, now a manager. His boxing gym is above the Cricketers' Arms: landlord Albert Cort, always known as Fatal because everything that happens to him or near him is 'fatal for business.' If beer prices go up, good punters die; if road works or demolitions start near the pub. . . all are used as a reason for reduced takings, he never considers the fact that he is drunk most of the time.

Fatal has a neurotic wife named Doris who's seen better days which were no doubt during the war when American troops were everywhere. She's recently altered her name to Doríce and now wishes to be addressed as such. This came about, in the opinion of the customers, because she's been voted onto the local Committee of the Licensed Victuallers for although Fatal is the licensee he's never been asked to join anything.

How the pub got the name *Cricketers' Arms* is a mystery as Harry has never heard cricket discussed even once in the twelve years he's been using the place. About a dozen boxers train five nights a week in the gym, with sometimes a weekend session if there's a bout arranged, but generally they come and go as they please outside of normal gym hours. All professionals with a few amateurs dropping in now and again for a workout, dodging the local vest-wearing brigade and their stuffy officials. Most of the pros are bottom of the bill fighters but do good business as late substitutes and fodder for the up and comers. They all seem to get into the pub bar before Harry.

Then there's Tommy Law, an American by birth, a former Golden Gloves Boxing Champion and a proud paratrooper during the war. While doing his D-Day training in England he married his 'Fair English Rose' as he always refers to her when drinking, but she'd cleared off with the local tally man before Tommy's jump boots had touched French soil. He lives nearby in one of the many houses long since condemned after the bombings but propped up and declared habitable while every one waits to be re-housed. He spends the early evening in the gym and then Fatal's public bar, mostly having a go at the boxers and customers or whoever is handy and grows more morose and bitter as the drink goes down and the night wears on. But he's a good trainer and knows the fight game.

'Hey Harry,' shouted an excited Tommy from across the gym. 'Remember that big leggy bird named Sarah, always sat on a bar stool with her skirt up around her arse? Well she reached her fucking level last night; down the road she came, on the arm of a local villain and a darkie at that! No offence meant to your lot, Chalky, it's just that I always had her for a slut.'

Harry and Chalky turned away and grinned at each other. Chalky Lewis, a skinny coloured welterweight from Jamaica; a nice kid who could make something of himself with more attention to gym work and less time chasing girls. Tommy had been fond of Sarah but got more drunk than usual one night, said a few choice words which started a row, and all hell broke loose. She reported Fatal to the police for not controlling his customers so he told her to 'fuck off and stay out of his pub.' Well. . . he couldn't bar Tommy!

'It was fun while it lasted,' remarked Harry as he looked across the gym to where one of the boxers was pounding the heavy bag.

'Hey Tony! I've got a fight for you next Tuesday on Sid Suthall's show at Brackley, a six rounder for good money. The kid's a banger so it's slip-and-slide, jab-and-grab night. Sid's short of bouts and needs a few rounds from you.'

'That's okay by me boss. How much?'

Harry swung around to face him growling. 'How fucking much! Do you mean how much you have on the book? Or what you walk away with?'

Tony looked sideways at him and replied quietly. 'Well as long as I draw enough to pay a few bills and shut the old woman up, that'll do.'

Harry walked to the only window in the gym, streaked with grime and cobwebs, he could just make out the railway station in the distance and thought what it would be like to take a long ride out of there.

§

The gym takes in the length and breadth of the pub's top floor. There are two entrances, one through the pub front door and up a flight of stairs which Fatal likes the boxers and hangers on to use early evening. It makes his establishment look busy. The rear entrance is through a double gate into a large back yard with a fire escape up to the gym. The boxers use the yard when it's clear of beer crates, barrels and debris mainly to get some fresh air and perhaps do a skip as smoke from the bar seeps up through the walls and ceilings into the gym.

Everyone leaves by the back way unless heading for the bar. Again this is Fatal's idea as he doesn't want people to be seen leaving his pub considering it bad for business.

To the rear of the yard and extending down one side of the pub is a waste area as many houses in the vicinity have been demolished leaving the ground empty while the council decide what to do with it.

The waste ground is now useful as a car park since some Gypsies had cut down the wire netting fence and pulled on a few caravans. The council, after initial protests, backed off deciding it was pointless to attempt repairs and they now turn a blind eye.

A long row of still-standing terraced properties adjoin the pub from the other side, now mostly lodging houses some privately owned, where Tommy and a few of the boxers have rooms. The council has taken over the rest and these are mostly filled up with dossers.

The top floor of the pub had originally been used at weekends for sing-songs and live entertainment with Doríce on the piano and a local drunk playing a string bass made out of a tea chest. But this did not last long with fights breaking out and people falling down the steep stairs.

Harry had always been a regular at the Cricketers' which was where he met Tommy. They'd began training boxers in the local Memorial Hall but with complaints from neighbours about the noise and bad language the council gave them notice and were only too pleased to see the pub 'Club Room' let for use as a box-ing gym.

Fatal has the pub premises on a long lease from the council so the presence of the gym gave his business a boost. It has the usual equipment with heavy bags, speed balls and a good sized ring which is a lot better than they'd had in the Memorial Hall where a rope around four chairs had to do.

Various bits and pieces had arrived via donations; the lockers came from the council and much of the rest from Jack the Lads who like being around the boxing scene. Posters of long gone boxing shows are gradually peeling off the walls and there's a sink in the corner with a cold water tap. The toilet, however, is downstairs and out the back yard, which is the same for the pub clientele, often causing friction and an exchange of cheeky remarks followed by the occasional punch up.

A posh gym doesn't make champions. It helps, but that's all.

§

Harry's childhood had been anything but easy. Father, Len, had enlisted in the army at the outbreak of the Great War with so many of his chums and had survived until the Battle of Loos when an exploding shell took off his right arm below the elbow. Finally discharged with a measly pension he'd immediately campaigned to the highest level, demanding to know why an officer's arm was worth nearly twice as much as a private's when disability pensions were calculated. He was fobbed off with excuses and his efforts came to nothing.

He'd married his childhood sweetheart, Clara, in 1919 and Harry was born the following year and then in quick succession, Reginald and Mavis. By the time the great depression set in there were children to support as well as an ailing wife. It was difficult for Len to hold down a job, not just because of his disability but more to do with his irascible and aggressive nature.

A job opportunity came his way from the local vicar to act as watchman for the church and outbuildings as youths tended to congregate there and sometimes caused damage. Len was told to have a quiet word with them when possible and point out that the waste ground nearby was better suited for their games. After a heavy drinking session in his local pub he grabbed the ringleader one afternoon and threatened to slam his hob nailed boot up his arse four lace holes if he didn't bugger off with all his pals. This exchange of words was overheard by the vicar and as it hardly followed his suggested verbal instructions it was back on the dole for Len, which was unfortunate as his straight forward approach stopped any further problems from the local youth.

Clara died of consumption in 1936 and although Len was still bitter over his treatment by the military authorities he finally agreed to young Harry joining the army as a boy soldier. Sidney joined up a year later. With just Mavis at home life became a little easier for Len and gave him more time for his drinking which by now had taken over his life.

Harry was serving in Palestine with the Royal Engineers when news of his father's death reached him and he arrived back in England shortly before war was declared. A visit to Mavis who had gone into service and was happy working in a grand house, then he was off to France. He got out at Dunkirk and decided to transfer to the Bomb and Mine Disposal Unit, just in time for the blitz. He ended the war as a sergeant with a medal (which was in his desk drawer) for 'special work'. He never talks about why it was given to him and rarely mentions his service in England, but occasionally jokes about his time in Europe, which he says was more of a holiday.

Then there is Yvonne or 'Vonnie' as Harry calls her. A quick marriage early in the war, a husband killed while fighting in the desert and along came Harry. He should have married her but used the old, 'best wait until the war is over,' scenario to put things off. So she married a young army officer who turned out to be a right pig and by the early nineteen fifties it was all finished and back came Harry.

Vonnie lives in a smart house the other side of Whitton and Harry is welcome any time: providing he's sober. In reality he always seems to gravitate back to his few rooms near the pub. Vonnie moans and groans at him, but she's resigned to the *status quo*. Still an attractive looking woman, she knows it's always going to be Harry for her from now on.

2

'We'd better take Chris with us next Tuesday, Tom,' Harry shouted from the gym office. 'Sid telephoned and said he might be short of another bout! And make sure his licence is in order, you know what an arsehole the Board official is. This is a good turnout for early evening so get all the subs in. And no hard luck stories!'

'Okay Harry, all will be done.' grunted Tommy, with little enthusiasm.

The gym was busy with boxers in various training routines when Tommy stopped suddenly from fixing up a speed ball and with a puzzled look on his face strolled over toward where Harry was sifting through some papers.

'What's that fucking noise coming from downstairs?' he quizzed.

Harry burst out laughing. 'It's Fatal and Doríce, pissed. They've just got back from a pub committee lunch, all airs and graces from her with her cigarette holder, prancing around kissing all the men. And Fatal. . . what a fucking mess! Shirt burst open showing his fat gut and his navel stuck out like a pig's ear.'

'Well who's behind the bar?' quizzed Tommy, looking concerned.

'Big Gladys with Eric helping her,' replied Harry, trying hard to keep a straight face.

'Eric helping her?' shouted Tommy. 'Helping his fucking self you mean! He'll be paralytic by nine o'clock.'

Everybody liked young Eric but failed to really understand his illness and generally put his erratic behaviour and occasional collapses down to the amount of strong drink he consumes.

Suddenly Harry looked concerned and sidling quietly up to Tommy whispered. 'Yes Tom, we'd better call in the bar after the gym, a bit smartish. I heard Micky say he was meeting Danny and some mates there for a drink later and you know how those Gypsies can play up.'

Harry knew his boxers, Micky Casey, a Gypsy boy with great talent but an erratic lifestyle, he could go places but no doubt will end up camp fire talk like most of them. He took a long hard look at the sparring but said nothing thinking about the old days and what might have been. He knew he had talent in the gym, so maybe it was him getting it wrong; perhaps he should have got out years ago. Times were changing and the fight business wanted more reliable boxers with disciplined trainers and managers.

'Well bollocks to it all,' he muttered. 'Where else can I find anyone like Tommy to drink with me.'

§

'It's no wonder customers fall down these stairs; with or without a fucking drink,' remarked Tommy. 'The hand rail's been loose for years; that fat, lazy bastard Fatal needs to get his hammer and nails working.'

Harry locked the door and carefully followed Tommy. With each step the noise from the bar increased. Suddenly they are in and it's bedlam. Fatal is flat out across two benches with no sign of Doríce. Micky and his cronies are at the far end of the bar. Big Gladys is doing her best with little success as Eric is in the state Tommy said he would be and gave Harry a frozen stare when asked where Doríce was.

Gladys turned from the till for a moment and shouted over the hubbub. 'She went out with Erwin some time ago.'

Erwin Samos, a coffee coloured Jamaican who thinks he is the new calypso king. He's been having it off with Doríce for months and everybody in the pub knows except perhaps Fatal, or maybe he just doesn't care.

Harry looked around at the mass of faces in case any dodgy ones have slipped in knowing that Fatal was flat out and Doríce missing. All seemed alright so he edged towards Micky who was showing his mate Danny his latest sucker punch. Harry playfully separated them like a referee and pulled him to one side.

'I want you to keep an eye on this place until closing time Mick, Fatal's had it and Doríce is otherwise engaged, Tommy will be here, is that okay?'

'Sure Harry, me and the boys will hang around until closing time.'

'Good Mick, see you tomorrow.'

Tommy was already on his second pint when he felt Harry's hand on his shoulder, 'I'm off in a minute Tom; I've had a long day. Micky will be staying, I gave him some responsibility so he and his mob will behave. He'll help you get Fatal upstairs but I would leave him where he is until closing time and it's best to get Eric into my taxi - we don't want him having a fit amongst this lot; not that any of them would notice. Gladys will cash up and lock the till. Christ knows when Doríce will be back. Hopefully never!'

'Okay, no problem,' muttered Tommy, 'but what a fucking carry on!'

§

'You look happy this morning Albert, Doríce died in her sleep?'

'Cut out the fucking smart talk Coupon. . . my Doríce does a lot of good work around here.'

'Yes', thought Coupon, 'mostly flat on her back.'

Stanley Edgar Wall, better known as Swerving Stan the Coupon Man, is a tired out old Spiv. Having dodged call-up during the war and avoided the Home Guard, he was seen on occasions wearing an ARP helmet and now leads the Remembrance Day Parade, proudly displaying a medal. How he'd obtained this medal no one knew. Coupon had grown up with Fatal and they'd loyally remained at each others' throats.

21

He was expected to hang himself when rationing had finally ended and the black market had disappeared. Instead he bought a few of the terraced houses alongside the pub and despite the fact that they had since been condemned and were scheduled for demolition he rents out the rooms. Tommy and some of the boxers are his tenants and the few quid he gets from them and his various other dealings keeps him going. Coupon recently became a ticket man for the fights but will still supply almost anything: no names, no pack drill. However, like his surroundings, Swerving Stan has become somewhat shabby.

'Now listen Albert, this television business is all the talk and you need one in your bar, it will pack the place out. Teddy Long has signed a contract with a big city promoter who has the television contract to put on weekly fights so there is going to be money for everyone.'

'Okay yes,' replied Fatal, 'but what does Harry think about all this wheeling and dealing? You know he fell out with Teddy over Sid passing Kenny Cole on to him and now he's the champion.'

'Well,' jumped back Coupon, 'the kid owed Sid so much money and he had the main share so to get straight he had to get rid of him. Harry came out of it alright, Sid squared him up and he made on the deal, anyway they all need to work together now as it's looking good.'

Fatal gave Coupon a long hard look. 'How much is this TV going to cost me? I don't want another performance like the fucking pin ball machine. . . the police calling for it the next day. Doríce went mad.'

'Now look Albert,' said Coupon, who always called Fatal by his baptismal name when business was being conducted and money was involved, 'that was an unfortunate misunderstanding and I can guarantee this is all on the level. Don't pay me a penny, just try it for a week.'

Fatal frowned, 'I'll have a word with Doríce, she doesn't want any trouble with the law as she's just been voted on to the pub committee and trouble like that happening again will give those two faced bastards ammo against her.'

'Good man Albert,' replied a now chirpy Coupon, 'you could always see a great business opportunity when it arrived, it will be up and running by the weekend, in the meantime you can put Harry in the picture. Picture! Never mind. See you tonight.'

§

Harry couldn't understand why he had the feeling of a mighty hangover when he'd had so few drinks the night before.

Perhaps as Tommy always said it was the prospect of meeting Teddy Long again. There is always some friction when boxers change managers and that had been the case with Kenny Cole. Tommy found him and brought him through the amateurs, Harry got him a professional licence and did a deal with Sid Suthall on the promotional side. . . and that was when the trouble started.

Good in the gym and in the ring but a nightmare otherwise, Kenny spent money like a sailor paid off ship, all his earnings and all he could borrow. Soon he was into Sid and Harry too deep and had to go. In comes Teddy and four fights later Kenny is British Champion, with Sid and Harry looking on. The only one who didn't seem to mind his going was Tommy who still reckons there are chinks in his armour but it will take a good fighter to beat him. As part of the deal it was agreed that should Kenny win the title he would make his first defence, a voluntary one, on a Sid Suthall promotion and that was the following Tuesday with TV coverage; not that Harry's fighters, on the undercard, would be screened but it was a start.

A side room off from the gym and across the landing is used by Harry as his office; just a desk, a bench and a few chairs, with a metal cabinet to house all the mail from the Board and keep a check on the boxers as best he can. His diary is his Bible and contains all personal information, and most importantly the money owed him by the boxers. An old black telephone in the centre of the desk always has a lock on it to stop the boxers using it when Harry is out and the office left open.

Tommy's head appeared around the door. 'Guess what? A television set has just been delivered downstairs. Coupon's in there helping to fix it up behind the bar. It's got to be Doríce's idea; Fatal would never think of it. Do we get any more money if our fighters are screened?'

Harry looked up, 'I don't know. That'll be Sid Suthall's business and he'll take every penny he can; particularly from Teddy who I understand is in on the promotion. Well, he has the top of the bill fighter and he's champion. . . and Tom, don't steam into Teddy, at least not until after we draw our money.'

'No worry,' muttered an exasperated Tommy. 'It's just that he took all the glory when Kenny won the title and done fuck all for him apart from getting him the shot; which he would have got anyway with us.'

'All water under the bridge now Tom,' replied a relieved Harry forcing a smile. 'Now go and find us another champion.'

3

'By the way Tom, make sure Tony and Chris are here at the pub next Tuesday by twelve noon, the weigh in is at two. Sid's arranged a room for you and the boys to put your feet up and some grub if you want any. It's part of the deal so don't listen to anyone asking for money.'

Tommy nodded his head, 'Is there a few pounds lee way when we're on the scales as you haven't told me what weight the fights have been made at and I don't want a flare up with the Board inspector.'

Harry slapped Tommy on the back and smiled, 'Tom, there will be no problems, just get there on time and weigh them in and look don't let Chris talk you into giving his bird a lift. You know the trouble we had before with her getting in his room when you were out; in the fucking pub as it happened.'

'Come on Harry I only turned my back for a few minutes and in she slipped. If Chris was as cunning in the fucking ring he might last the distance more often.'

'Alright Tom just do your best with them. I'll see you at the weigh-in, as I've made arrangements with Willie my taxi driver, to run me there and then take me back to Whitton. He'll drop me off around six o'clock at your hotel before starting his shift. Tony is on first and Chris after the interval. We'll stay and watch Kenny who shouldn't take too long to get rid of Don Bell . . . anyway he deserves an easy first defence.'

Tom nodded again. 'I need a few quid Harry to see me over in case of bits and pieces. We can sort out everything else later.' Harry looked hard at Tommy. 'Bits and fucking pieces? It's an hour's drive to Brackley with no stops. so what's the problem?'

Tommy looked hurt and turned away growling. 'Bollocks to it then. Let's go and see how Fatal is doing with his new toy.'

Harry followed him down the stairs after carefully locking the office door. The pub bar had just opened, the so called lounge stayed shut during lunchtime but usually had a few people in at night. Fatal was standing on a chair twiddling knobs on the television set which was balanced on a piece of board nailed to the spirit shelf.

'Doríce!' he shouted. 'Doríce, turn the aerial the other way. That's it! we've got a picture!'

Dorice entered the bar, brushing haughtily past Harry and Tommy and stood gloating at the new toy.

'You must appreciate, I am sure, that one has to keep up with the times. Which, of course, will help create more interest in your boxing business; at no extra cost to you I may add. It will be packed in here next week. . . a shame you let Kenny go. The second one you've lost. Still, we can only hope you manage to find another champion.'

Harry thought Tommy was about to hit her and ushered him to the corner of the bar. Fatal clambered back onto the floor as Doríce sauntered out and muttered apologetically. 'She don't really mean any harm. In fact she never liked Kenny. . . but young Billy, well, that was a different matter. A couple of pints gentlemen?'

§

Billy Stone had been an evacuee from London very early in the war to escape the bombing and when it was time for him to return to his young mother she was nowhere to be found. Extensive investigations proved fruitless as she'd simply disappeared like so many did in those terrible days. Having no known relatives Billy was fostered out and subsequently passed from one family to another as circumstances changed. Life was very hard for him and at the age of fifteen he joined a Merchant Navy training vessel, became a deck hand and found that life aboard ship gave him new found friends and stability in his life.

He drifted into boxing on the booths between voyages and everyone soon told him he could have a future ashore as a fighter so he left the Merchant Navy. He'd spent some of his time on leave with a pal who lived in Whitton and they often talked about the local boxing club. At the time Harry and Tommy also trained some amateurs until the fuddy duddy officials warned them off. They simply got a registered amateur trainer, said he used the gym at different times to the professionals, and that was that. Billy joined.

He proved a good amateur winning a national title but his face didn't fit with the hierarchy and he was overlooked repeatedly by the England team selectors. Billy's fighting style was more suited to the professional game; unlimited stamina, he could box on the front and back foot, with a knockout wallop in his right hand, and more, he could take a punch. He soared through his six round fights after turning pro at nineteen and was soon knocking on the door of seasoned fighters. Then came the big one, a title shot and they had a champion at last.

Hardly a day goes by without Harry thinking of what might have been if they'd all travelled home together but he'd wanted a drink at the venue with supporters, so Tommy and the rest of the boys left in Harry's taxi leaving him with Billy, basking in their great achievement. Billy was slumped in the passenger seat of the van, and fast asleep, by the time Harry returned to drive home. Normally Billy would have rested in the back of the van but it was full of kit.

Although Harry had very little to drink compared to even an average night, he felt he'd had enough and slightly stumbled before climbing into the driver's seat. Somewhere along the road he must have dozed off and remembers nothing until he woke up in hospital. Harry was not badly hurt but Billy was dead.

Somehow Harry had been flung clear and they found Billy wedged under the driver's seat so the coroner decided he must have been driving and an accident was recorded. Harry said nothing at the inquest, well it wouldn't have brought his fighter back but what happened has hung over him ever since like a heavy black shroud. He never told anyone the truth about that night but Vonnie and certainly Tommy have an idea what really happened. Everyone else just muttered and nodded when the verdict came out.

All those years of hard work and finally you reach the top with a fighter and in a flash it's all over.

§

'Now look Tom, keep the key to the motor on you at all times and if the boys don't want to use the room Sid has for them and would sooner rest up in the van you let them in; but keep the key. You know what Chris is like and might persuade Tony to use the room to put his feet up and then get his bird in the van. We don't want another fucking spectacle like before with punters walking by and gawping at him and a half naked girl in my van with "Harry Keys Boxing Team" painted on the side of it. I still get cheeky comments from arseholes. . . I don't know how that fucking Chris copes with it all. We need six rounds from him tonight.'

'Okay Harry I'll keep my eye on everything, mumbled Tommy as he turned away, 'and I'm glad I painted out that fucking sign.'

The boxers weighed in with no fuss and even the Board official seemed in a good mood. Tommy had a quick word with Kenny Cole who seemed in high spirits and looking forward to the first defence of his title. His opponent was hand-picked by Teddy Long as it was a voluntary defence and there was little doubt that Kenny would skate through it.

Harry nodded to Teddy and shook his hand, somewhat reluctantly, as did Tom who had strict instructions to behave himself. Sid had even lost that look of complete panic which promoters seem to have at weigh-ins and invited all the various managers and officials back to his office for a drink and a snack. Tommy disappeared with Tony and Chris to the room provided by Sid so Harry went back to his taxi, alone with his thoughts and Willie drove him back to his rooms in Whitton.

§

As arranged Harry stopped off at the hotel on his return, wished the boys good luck and told them to listen to Tom at all times then left to make his way to the venue. It was filling up with the usual early punters and posers ringside; lots of hand-shakes and nods with some friendly remarks about Kenny Cole and some not so friendly. Kenny had a good following and was a ticket seller, apart from Gypsy Micky all Harry's fighters turned up carrying their bag to make up the bill, but that was how it all was.

Tony was first on following the dreary announcements and jabbed and moved taking no chances against an up and coming boxer in the Teddy Long camp. Caught by a looping right hand now and again he was not otherwise troubled and did just enough to please Sid the promoter, making sure he lasted the distance so could go out again as soon as he was needed.

Raising his opponent's hand at the end was a formality and Sid gave Harry a friendly punch on the arm as he passed by on his way ringside. 'One up and one to go Harry. Just the job,' he whispered.

Harry looked around the almost full hall, the one where Billy had won his title and thought how he was now back to six round fighters padding out the show; life for him had certainly turned into a mean street.

After the interval Chris did his usual running act for six rounds and was out of the ring almost before the announcer read out the details of his points defeat.

Kenny stopped his opponent in the sixth round after holding him up for the previous two, making a show of it all for the tel-evision cameras with Teddy and Sid hardly able to contain themselves, back slapping and smiling at all and sundry. Harry collected his fighters' wages with the usual argument over ver-bally agreed expenses, so rarely written into the contracts and then they were in the van and heading back to see Fatal.

§

'Where *was* everybody Harry? Never a sign of you!' bellowed Fatal as they entered the packed bar. 'Kenny looked good. He'll be a champ for a long time.'

'Yeah, he did well,' said Harry with a combined smile and a grimace as Tommy burst out laughing, having spotted Eric slumped on a stool in the corner of the bar.

'At least Eric's had a good time by the look of him,' shouted Tommy over the babble of voices. 'Now let's have some drinks Fatal. Four pints will do nicely and good to see the television works!'

4

'Great success then Albert,' said a beaming Coupon as he walked into the bar. Fatal stopped stacking the shelves and sat on his stool. 'Yes, yes, good crowd. Now I suppose you want some money?'

'Just twenty quid on account for now and we can. . .'

That was as far as he got as Doríce glided through the doorway reeking of cheap perfume.

'Thank you Stanley,' she quickly interrupted. 'I will take care of the financial dealing from now on. Albert tends to lose track of what he's paid out.'

'That's fine by me Doríce. Twenty notes will keep me going and of course I will give you a receipt.'

'Of course. . . but one moment please Stanley, I must discuss some pub business with my husband.'

'Albert, I was embarrassed at the performance of the boxing crowd in this bar last night. You must have a word with Harry about Tommy as he was drunk again and play fighting with that awful Gypsy Micky. What with money changing hands and foul language my friends from the pub committee were shocked.'

Albert looked up with disinterest. 'Well Doríce they spend a load of money as always and your little lot never got rid of two bob. If we had to depend upon them for takings it would be fatal. Next time you'd best take your 'friends' into the lounge.'

Doríce visibly bristled. 'Albert, you refuse ever to hear a bad word about that mob from upstairs. If you recall I did try the lounge after last month's meeting but you sent in Eric to serve us who promptly had one of his fits. He nearly bit off Cedric's finger as he administered first aid. It can't go on like this if we are trying to upgrade the place.'

Fatal let out a heavy sigh as he'd heard it all before. 'To be honest Doríce your crowd were more embarrassed by that chocolate drop boyfriend of yours joining the company, scrounging drinks and fawning over everyone. If he ever bought a drink his next would be the first!'

'How dare you refer to him in that way!' screamed Doríce, obviously offended. 'My committee friends are very fond of Erwin.' She bristled with pride. 'He's to appear on television, I hope you know, in the *American Discovery Show*. At least Erwin is trying to make something of his life, unlike your boxing lot.'

Coupon started clapping his hands sarcastically as Doríce flounced from the bar, spotting a chance to renew his efforts to acquire some money.

'Now, now, Albert, just a difference of opinion. These things happen all the time in pub life. I'd better have a quick half and my twenty notes before I get on my travels. Could you quickly put on the TV for the news: I hear there's trouble in the Middle East and hopefully those wogs will shut the canal and encourage petrol rationing.'

§

It was a rare occasion when Harry took Vonnie out anywhere other than Fatal's pub. She put up with it but the rough ways of the boxers and their drinking and mounting aggression as the evening wore on frightened her.

Tonight they were in the Taj Mahal the newly opened Indian restaurant in Whitton. They'd been there on the first evening as Jack, the owner, was an avid boxing fan. Of course Jack wasn't his real name but it would do and saved cheeky comments from all and sundry as Indians were still fairly scarce around the area.

'Hello Harry; and hello Yvonne. So good to see you both. Harry, you will soon find another champion, you see.' Harry smiled and nodded as Vonnie picked up the menu.

'Some of your boys were in here the other night,' Jack continued. 'That Micky and Danny with a few others; you know they spend like no tomorrow, but Harry, perhaps you could mention to them not to tell too many jokes about Indians out loud. No big problem, Harry but Danny kept calling the waiters 'Gunga Din' and saying, 'glad when your head gets better.' The waiters of course do not understand what he is saying but I am most embarrassed.'

'Christ those Gypsies at it again,' thought Harry.

'Don't worry Jack I'll take care of it first thing tomorrow and it won't happen again.'

'Many thanks to you Harry. Please don't stop them coming in as they spend plenty of money, but just to be a little quiet.'

Vonnie looked up as Jack motioned a waiter over to their table.

'I really don't know how you put up with those Gypsies, Harry. They're constantly in trouble; what with Micky fighting in the street and Danny always in the newspaper for doing something illegal.'

'Well they are what they are and nothing will change them,' grunted a tiring Harry.

Suddenly he realised the other licensed fighters were due back in the gym. Harry traditionally sent as many of his boxers as he could to his mate Ronnie's travelling boxing booth on the fair ground for a few weeks during the summer. It kept them fit with a few quid in their pockets and a small amount back to Harry as commission. He had Ronnie's note with him and pulled the crumpled sheet of paper out of his pocket, spreading it across the table, moving Vonnie's wine glass out of the way to make room. He noted that Sam, Dickie, Johnny and Jake were on their way back, and he smiled when he read Ronnie's PS.

Harry read it out loud: 'Brett has got mixed up with a Tropical Dancer and would be staying a while.' He always lost one or two in this way but they found their way back eventually.

Harry looked up and noticed the harsh look on Vonnie's face, 'Harry, just for one evening can you please forget about boxing?'

§

'Sure Joe, of course I can do one side of the bill for you; the boys have just returned from the booth. They're fully fit. I'll send the

33

details off today. The Irish kid Brett will be on the bill. . . I know he's a favourite with your punters.'

'That's great Harry, just don't include the Gypsy kid Micky. I don't want anything to do with him after the punch up involving his gang last time.'

'No worries Joe, I know the score with your shows.'

Harry put the phone back and walked into the gym.

It was a good turnout for training with all the active boxers there except Brett, the wild Paddy, but he would soon turn up.

'Tommy, we'll be doing one side of the bill at Joe Hardy's Stag Show on the 28th of this month. Tell Sam, Dicky, Jake and Brett - when he turns up - that they'll be boxing. No opponents yet, but no problem there as most are from Arthur Eldon's gym. All he has is losers.'

'What about me then Harry?' chirped Micky who had listened to the exchange of words. 'I could do with a nice easy night.'

'He doesn't want you nor your mob after the performance last time,' barked Harry.

'Now wait a minute boss.' retorted an obviously annoyed Mick. 'That rugby crowd were chanting cheeky comments at Danny's table and when his bird June climbed into the ring with the raffle tickets they rushed the ropes to look up her skirt. If that wasn't enough they then pelted everyone with bread rolls. Joe agreed afterwards it was them that started it all. Pound to a shilling those stuck up bastards still get a table.'

'Well,' replied Harry, knowing full well that what Micky said was correct, 'nothing I can do. It's Joe's show and he makes the rules and if he doesn't want you that's the end of it.'

Harry never liked dinner shows although they were good money and an easy night's work. A few real boxing fans but mostly posers, to fill up the ring leader's table, intent on getting pissed as quickly as possible. It was often gone midnight when they all got away but no real problem as Joe promoted in Whitton at the Granby Hotel the other side of town. Apart from the fracas the highlight of his last show was when the comedian laid out a heckler who invaded the ring during his act.

'I'll leave it all with you Tom and in the meantime I'll ring around to see what's happening for the next few months. Before

I do, you're not going to believe it but Jack Silver's got a manager and promoter's licence from the Board and is now up and away with *Main City Promotions*. And. . . wait for it, he's just signed a contract to put boxing on national television.'

Tommy looked up from bandaging Chalky's hands. 'How the hell did he get in after all he's been up to over the years. I thought the Board vetted everybody for villainy. Rubbish of course, Jack and his little lot would never have passed a test. As usual, scum rises to the fucking top and closes over everything. Anyway, I never trusted those bastards who keep smiling while they talk.'

'Well,' muttered Harry with a shrug of his shoulders, 'he's right in and has already been on the phone to Teddy and Sid offering his support for local shows. I suppose it means plenty of work for boxers but you can't trust the bastard - he's always whispering in their ears, especially if they're any good.'

Tommy gave a loud laugh. 'If that's his game there won't be much fucking whispering going on here. This lot are hardly championship material!'

The pained expression on Chalky's face and looks from the others stopped Tommy in his tracks.

'Alright, alright. . . maybe some of you could get there but keep going as you are and all you'll end up with is a nose like a cobbler's thumb and go stumbling about on your fucking heels, and, what's worse. . . no fucking money!'

Chris stopped skipping and shouted across the gym. 'I haven't got any fucking money *now*!'

§

As the boxing season was now getting under way Harry and Tommy decided to get the boxers most likely to be active out early for some road work. Neither of them believed the boys when they said they were up and about at the crack of dawn so Tommy drove up to the pub in the van at 6 am, as arranged, and there was Micky, Tony, Chris and Chalky, all looking slightly bedraggled and somewhat unhappy to be up and about at this unearthly hour.

'I'm taking you lot to the park where I'll keep an eye on you so pile in and off we go,' he chortled, immediately pleased to see others feeling as rough as he did after his heavy drinking the previous evening.

The park at Whittton was spread over twenty two acres of mostly open ground with a boating lake, a few trees some shops and toilets. It was previously rough fields but the recreation movement after the war had done a good job with it.

As they passed an early morning runner Micky suddenly wound down the window and shouted. 'Look at this fat bastard running on the pavement. That's what your lot do in America, you give road work a bad name! It's all the cake and ice cream you eat! Never have a proper fucking meal!'

Tommy looked straight at Micky and grinned. 'Leave him alone, the poor sod's trying his best. And as for a proper meal, you can talk with you lot eating fucking hedge hogs and anything else that crawls into your camp. Don't fucking shout at the poor slob, he might be a copper or something.'

'Well. . .' Micky muttered, winding up the window, 'he'll probably drop fucking dead in a few minutes anyway.'

The boxers always enjoyed these slanging matches, and felt more relaxed as the van turned into the park. They were soon off around the track at a steady pace, it was a beautiful morning and Tommy suddenly felt that perhaps his fortunes were about to change for the better.

5

Tommy watched them closely as they came back into view. Tony, who is in the lead, has a nagging, fat, ugly wife at home named Megan with two bone chilling kids who always seemed to be eating something. The girl is a small, perfectly formed version of her mother and the boy, well, Christ knows where he came from. He possesses the biggest head anyone has ever seen on a five year old child, which lolls one way then the other. Micky mentioned it one evening during a boxer family get together in Fatal's lounge bar and before Tony could intervene Megan head butted him. It transpired she has some Gypsy blood in her too, and after that performance she is given a wide berth by everyone. She never fails to rant and rage at Harry and Tommy about Tony's injuries and the money she claims he is never paid, and nothing changes. Tommy said it's no wonder Tony had turned to religion for help.

Chris Metzner, who had a German father, is a quiet type who likes the girls. Boxing to him is just a way of earning a few quid to see him through his studies. Chris missed call-up for National Service because of a deformed chest and he's known as the only hunch front in pro boxing. Nevertheless, he passed his medical with no problems, the Board doctor thinking he was just over developed. He is rarely spared when Tommy is feeling rough, or fed up with everything as he is now.

'And Chris, don't keep moaning about us spelling your fucking name wrong. With a Nazi as a father no wonder you get hissed at when they announce you. What a fucking state of affairs, Brits and everybody fighting for their freedom and the fucking Kraut prisoners are here on the farms eating good grub and shagging all the weeping widows. In my opinion we should have shot the fucking lot of the arrogant bastards when we had the chance.' The war had been over more than a dozen years but bitterness still rankled in Tommy's gut. 'They even let the blond haired, flat headed bastard into the British Legion Club! Fuck all that forgive and forget bollocks. Fatal had the right idea when he told him to goose step out of his fucking pub.'

Chris had heard it all before. His mother had been verbally abused when she married Heinz Metzner after he was released from the prisoner of war camp and decided to stay in England with Chris taking on the Metzner surname. People could hardly hide their glee when he died not long after from wounds received during the battle for Normandy. When Tommy is really on form he claims it was him who 'shot the bastard.' It was only after Heinz died that Isabel, Chris's mother, told him the truth about his father. It transpired Isabel came from wealthy farming stock and attended a prominent fee paying girl's school in the mid nineteen thirties. On a school trip to the Bavarian Alps she fell hopelessly in love with Heinz who was acting as guide for the holiday party. After returning to England she found she was pregnant by him and all his efforts to leave Germany and join her in England were blocked by the authorities. Her wealthy family decided she should have the baby and she left the farm to stay with relatives many miles away. In those days getting pregnant outside marriage was a terrible disgrace and but for her family's money she would have been sent to a special home and probably never heard of again. As the political situation in Europe deteriorated Isabel lost touch with Heinz and his letters stopped and hers were returned. Heinz immediately wrote to Isabel when he arrived at the prisoner of war camp in England and they exchanged letters until his release. After hearing the true story Chris was more than ever determined to keep his German surname.

Chalky: well, what can be said about him? He's there for the money and the local publicity he gets from being a boxer. After training, on goes his white suit and a hat the size of an Indian tepee and he's out on the town; chasing girls, preferably white ones.

Then there's Micky. So much talent but a totally erratic and unreliable individual. Too much bare knuckle fighting at Gypsy fairs and larking about. He goes missing for days then turns up at the gym as though nothing has happened. Promoters love him as he sells bundles of tickets but are wary of his wild and noisy followers so always try to get him a win. Tommy knew Micky could go places. He had all the ingredients to make a champion but it just wasn't enough.

It wasn't as if any of the boxers had a steady income from day jobs, Chalky did a bit of roofing and general building but spent most of his time with his girlfriends. Chris put in a few hours at the local college tending the boilers and general maintenance. Gypsy Micky's source of funds can only be imagined and the same with Sam and Dicky. Tony was on the dole and having to sign on three times a week prevented him doing much else. Not that he was keen to do anything except dodge his nagging wife. Brett seemed to be the only one who had a legitimate income from his self-employed gardening business. Although orders for work were erratic he managed to give Jake and Johnny the occasional day's work while trying to put a few quid Tony's way. Megan, of course, put a stop to that accusing Brett of using work as an excuse to arrange a booze up. Brett did go on the occasional spree which often lasted a couple of days, but then he would abstain for weeks on end.

Tommy had his yankee army pension having been wounded in Normandy and this worked out pretty good for spending in England as apart from his drinking he had few expenses. He also did a stint on the door of the local night club if there were no boxing commitments.

Harry had bought two taxi cabs some years before and had a good income from them although it came with the inevitable problems of finding reliable drivers, especially for the night shift.

Their way of life enabled all of them to be free at a few hour's notice should a call come from the boxing fraternity with offers of work.

Tommy began shouting at Jake before he had even stripped and started training.

'We had a call from Ralph Grimes. You boxed on his last show and he complained you argued with the Whip when he called you on. The man was only doing his job, so what the fuck was it all about?'

Jake looked up with a bored expression on his battered face. 'He told me I'd be on after the interval, then suddenly called me early with no notice because some bastard hadn't turned up. I wasn't ready.'

'Never mind all that 'not ready' bit, growled Tommy, now getting more agitated. 'We had to talk Ralph into taking the fight in the first place as you were six pounds over the agreed weight. Too much of the fucking barrack room lawyer in you. Now he doesn't want you on his shows.'

Jake shrugged his shoulders and muttered. 'Well he's a slimy shit anyway.'

'You can cut out the name calling!' bellowed a now steaming Tommy. 'He let you fight overweight and that's your fucking problem; we never know how you're going to be on the scales, your brother was a good prospect and look at him now: a great fat slob doing a market stall selling junk.'

This last outburst caused Jake to straighten up. 'Timmy has glandular trouble.'

'What?' shouted a laughing Tommy. 'Glandular? You don't go to bed weighing eleven stone and wake up weighing fucking fourteen. The problem was overtime on his knife and fucking fork. Eating all the time, straight from the gym. Fish and chips, or stuffing his gob with a meat and potato pie. You'll go the same fucking way, Jake, if you're not careful and I don't want to be wasting my time again.'

He turned away gasping for breath and saw Harry standing in the gym doorway trying to hide a smile. 'You forgot to mention the half-a-dozen pints Timmy sinks most nights in Fatal's bar! It's a hard game Tom, a hard game. We just have to keep going.'

Micky and Chalky are grinning, loving all this abusive cross talk. More often than not they are on the receiving end.

Everyone takes Tommy's outbursts with a pinch of salt; no nationality, colour, race, nor creed is excluded and there are no favourites with Tom.

Tony escapes most of this as his background is orphanages, reform school, and prison. So it has all been said and now he is a 'born again' Christian and often relates the story of how he wandered into a revival meeting in a drunken stupor and saw the light.

What he does get from Tommy when he drops to his knees in the ring before the opening round is. 'Cut out the Ace, King, Queen, and Jack routine. Say a prayer you don't get hit on the fucking chin or you'll see more lights than in Piccadilly Circus!'

§

It was Tommy who spotted him first standing at the top of the stairs and peering into Harry's office. He was casually dressed in a lumber jacket and what looked like army trousers and had a bag under his arm. Near six feet tall with closely cropped hair his face showed up strangely white as he stood under the naked light bulb hanging from the ceiling.

'What can I do for you?' he shouted.

'I'd like to join the gym. Are you the man I need to see. My name's Vic Lane?'

The conversation was cut short by Brett's appearance in the doorway and the bedlam that this provoked among the other boxers.

'Hello! He's back from the Islands. Mr Fucking Yakki Hula. Where is she then, your so-called Tropical Dancer?' Dicky shouted at the top of his voice as they all began an Hawaiian dance across the floor.

Brett mumbled and grunted and looked bedraggled. 'She wasn't Hawaiian; she was from Merthyr Tydfil. And her husband turned up, a fucking great coal miner so I got out of there smartish. Left all my money on the table and had to hitch hike back.'

Tommy burst out laughing, 'I told you to steer clear of those fucking Yantos, bus loads of the nutters cross over the border into England every Sunday because their pubs are shut and get drunk and start fights. Trust a thick Paddy like you to fuck it up.'

Brett grinned, sat down and replied wearily. 'Well I'm back now, hope you've got some work for me Tom. Is Harry in? I need a sub.'

Tommy still smiling, shouted at Brett. 'Get on with some training as you are fighting at the end of this month, Harry's not in and when he does come back don't go pestering him straight away for a sub.'

He was sure he'd seen this new kid before somewhere but couldn't place him. Then again he'd seen so many. 'The boss is out at the moment. What have you been doing with yourself?'

The lad crossed into the gym giving it a cursory look with no change of expression. 'I've just come out of the army. . . done some boxing there.'

Now Tommy had him. He'd got to the national amateur final at welterweight and lost a very dodgy points decision. 'Yeah I remember you in the championships. You were robbed. . . so what are you doing now and why come to this gym?'

'I saw your Billy Stone fight a few times and he came to my final. We chatted a lot, and he seemed happy with everything here. Terrible what happened to him; he would have been around a long time.'

'Yeah,' grunted Tommy, his face saddened at the mention of Billy's name, 'you'll have to see Harry Keys, the boss. He'll be back later, strip off and look around and have a workout but no sparring.'

Vic nodded, and Chalky showed him to an empty locker, 'Welcome to this fun house mate and if you can fight, no problems. Take no notice of Brett, he's just a mad Paddy.'

He was soon stripped off and loosening up with a few bends and twists. He looked more like a middleweight now but was carrying no extra pounds, and began on the heavy bag, moving quickly around throwing jabs and hooks. Vic looked good. . . but didn't they all on a bag? Tommy recalled watching Vic's fight in the final. He had his opponent down a couple of times but failed to finish him. As a pro he would have more of a chance, with the ref not interfering all the time.

He heard someone coming up the creaking stairs. It was Harry, reeking of booze and much the worse for wear. He glanced into the gym on reaching the top and half-turning into the office, stopped. 'I see Brett's back but who's that other kid?'

'Vic Lane,' replied Tom. 'Just out of the army and wants to fight for us. . . needs a pro licence but has done a bit. I think we should give him a try.'

'Okay Tom I'll speak to him later, just keep an eye on him, we don't want any more loonies up here.'

6

After visiting various punters in an effort to get sponsorship for bouts on Joe's boxing promotion, Harry had arrived at mid-day for his arranged meeting with Sid Suthall at a small bar opposite the Granby Hotel, supposedly to discuss future fight promotion plans involving the new syndicate headed by Jack Silver. Sid described Jack as a 'fucking bucket man gone above his station.' Sure he'd started in the fight game at the bottom, even had a couple of fights but it wasn't for him. With a change of name to partially disguise his Jewish background he'd latched on to a successful outfit who had some good fighters.

'And now look at the bastard!' Sid had shouted at Harry, much to the consternation of the bar manager who had little interest or sympathy for boxers or boxing people. The boozing had dragged on with a final decision that they would go along with Jack using Teddy Long as the go between and see what happened.

§

After spotting Brett and asking Tommy about the new kid Harry thought he'd made it safely into his office but was spotted by Tony who strolled across to the office door.

'I need a few quid boss until my next fight, a tenner will tide me over, trouble at home again.'

Harry turned quickly, nearly falling over. 'Not you again after a sub! With what you have on the book you need to fight every fucking week; you came here without a penny in your pocket,

Coupon gave you some rooms, your family turned up and it's been money, money, fucking money ever since. You and your lot had seen more breakfast times than breakfasts before you got here. . . all on the fucking dole and bone fucking idle!'

'Okay then, make it a fiver.' Tony smiled and leant against the door post. 'That should shut Megan up for a few days.'

Harry stumbled into the office and crashed down into his chair, confused and exhausted, just as Tommy's head appeared around the door. 'What the fuck was that all about? You could hear the shouting from down in the yard? By the look of you the meeting with Sid went well.'

Harry looked up as Tommy entered the office. 'Yeah, it all went well but you'd never believe these local business people and the answers I get when asking about sponsorship. The Ities at the restaurant wouldn't give anybody a free shock if they were a family of fucking ghosts; and yet Solly the Jewboy puts his hand in his pocket pronto, every time. No trouble at all.'

Tommy grinned. 'And those greasy hair-combing bastards fought *against* us in the war; that is until it started to go wrong. They're lucky to be here.'

Harry lent back in his chair and closed his eyes. Tom, showing unusual enthusiasm, sat down on the bench and continued excitedly. 'This new kid, Harry. . . he looks okay! I saw him fight last year and he's a banger; just what we need to liven up everything.'

'We'll see Tom, we'll see,' replied Harry drowsily. 'I'll ring the Board and arrange his medicals. Best ask him if he has any money to pay for everything or we'll have to deduct it from his purses. Let's just hope he doesn't fuck off after one fight.'

'Okay,' mumbled Tom, as he slowly got up and crossed the landing into the gym. He'd expected more encouragement and was somewhat taken aback by Harry's lack of enthusiasm.

§

Chris and Tony were in a huddle with Brett, Chalky and Micky, the rest of the boxers were sat over near the window. 'What the fuck's going on here,' shouted Tommy, 'a board meeting? Or a fucking strike?'

Vic was at the sink splashing water over his face and turned slowly to look at Tom. Before he could say anything Micky was in front of Tom. 'This new kid took liberties sparring Brett and needs a fucking talking to.'

Tom took a step back. 'I told you lot *no sparring*! So who's running this fucking gym?'

Vic dried his face and looked at Tommy. 'It was my fault. . . I jumped in with Brett. He hadn't heard you say no sparring and I opened up when I shouldn't have. It won't happen again.'

Tommy glared at Vic but something more troubled him. What was this kid after? First day in a strange gym and he's at it. . .

'Well if you want to stay here you follow the rules, otherwise down the fucking stairs you go.'

'Okay Tommy,' he replied, 'and sorry Brett. I guess I better buy the first round in the bar later.'

All the boxers seemed to relax and gave Vic a nod or a thumbs up, except Micky, who sidled up to Tommy as he turned to go. 'Hey Tom, watch this Vic, he's something different and looks a hitter in a hurry.'

§

Harry remained slumped in his office chair thinking of his next move. With nine active boxers, plus a new kid and plenty of work for them, the future looked bright. Thoughts whirled around in his head, maybe he should give the Whitton Globe a ring and get their sports reporter down for a story; perhaps a feature on Vic Lane. On second thoughts he worried that too big a splash, too early, could upset the other boxers. Then, again, the publicity would be good for Fatal's business too.

He walked across the landing into the gym. 'Hey Tom! What do you think about getting the Globe sports reporter down here for a story? We're doing alright at the moment with a lot ahead of us?'

Tommy looked up. 'Sounds good to me Harry. As long as that faggot journalist keeps his distance.' Tom was surprisingly tolerant of other people's sexual orientation, often describing 'them' as being 'a little on the sentimental side.' But when it came to Adrian Close, of the Globe a latent homosexual Tommy bore a serious grudge. He'd threatened to thump the reporter after the Billy Stone disaster when he'd insinuated that drink may have played no small part in the tragedy, adding that the management and boxers seem to spend more time in the pub bar than in the gym.

'Now look Tom,' cautioned Harry, 'best let bygones be bygones and back off. He's all we've got locally and the bigger papers are only interested in up and coming champions. We have none of them at present.'

'Alright Harry. I'll keep out of it but tell him to bring a cameraman for a group shot. Perhaps one of Vic. . . he was a near amateur champion last year.'

'Fine,' Harry sounded relieved. 'I'll get on it straight away.' He made the call and set the visit up for the coming Friday with the story to run the following week, just in time for Joe Hardy's dinner show. Harry yawned and stretched and thought what it might be like to have a champion in the stable again. But such contemplation always dragged him down and he was reminded of the whisky bottle in his desk drawer.

§

By the time they shut the gym and headed downstairs it was nine o'clock. Harry was still feeling the effects of his afternoon boozing session but put on a brave face as always; he considered it a self-inflicted wound and had to make the most of it. Tommy led the way through the opened bar door and a crowded scene greeted them. Micky and his hangers-on were in their usual corner with a few of the boxers, now including Vic, making raucous laughter at someone else's expense. Fatal was grinning behind the bar with his arm around a very attractive young girl. 'Hey Harry, have a look at our new bar maid Rita. All the boys approve.' He turned the girl slightly as if she were a prize on a fairground stall. 'And what do you think Tommy?'

The girl blushed as all eyes turned towards her, including Tommy's. 'She's certainly a glamour puss,' thought Tom, 'and brightens the place up. But how long can she last in this fucking lunatic asylum.'

'Pleased to meet you darling,' said a smiling Tom as he stuck out his hand which she squeezed, giving him a beaming smile.
This little exchange set the mob in the corner hooting and cheering which in turn caused Rita to blush even more.
'Give us a couple of pints Fatal if you can tear yourself away from *training* the staff,' shouted Harry over the noise.
Tom stage whispered into Harry's ear. 'She won't last long with Doríce around. Big Gladys, with a face like the back of a bus, is more her cup of tea. And when Eric sees her he'll have a fit, but that's nothing unusual.'
Harry smiled and nodded.

They pushed their way through the crowd to the boxers in the corner and looking at Vic, Tommy said. 'Don't let these nutters lead you astray. You've seen how they start drinking well before us. And keep away from Micky or you won't be able to hit the ground with your hat.'
This set them all hooting again but Harry forced a grin knowing the full truth of Tommy's words. Probably he and Tommy were as much to blame as anyone, but that's how it was and has always been. . . so, too late to change anything now.
Just then Doríce appeared behind the bar and Fatal moved faster than lightning to distance himself from Rita.
'Albert!' snapped Doríce, as she turned her head and directed a withering look at Micky and the gang. 'I trust you've been showing Rita the ropes and explained to her that some of our customers are less well behaved and less educated than others.'
'I've put her in the picture Doríce and she's doing fine,' replied a cringing Fatal. 'Good crowd in tonight and it's still early.'

7

Vic had his medical and everything was in order which left Harry to complete the Board registration form and the boxer/manager contract. After he sent a message via Tommy, Vic was knocking on his office door which was closed - an unusual occurrence when the gym was open.

'Come in!' boomed a voice from inside and Vic pushed the door with his shoulder to enter what was a spruced up room with Harry sat upright behind his old wooden desk.

'Tom said you had your medical and there were no problems. Let me have the form and your birth certificate,' Harry said in a friendly tone.

Vic sat down on the bench in front of the desk and handed the forms over. Harry gave them a quick glance and continued. 'I have to register you with the Board and then there's the contract between you and me. I take twenty five per cent of every purse; but nothing from your first three fights except expenses for medicals and bits and pieces. I'll ask your answer.'

Suddenly an embarrassed look crossed Vic's face. He took a deep breath and blurted out nervously. 'Before we go on I have to tell you that I was a foundling and my date of birth is approximate. My name is the name given to me after I was found in *Victory Lane*. The number on the shop doorway I was left in was 28; so I became Victor Lane, born 28th October 1936. I can't tell you any more than that. It's all there on my birth certificate.'

Harry looked up from the form and could see Vic was uneasy. 'No problem at all,' he replied with a smile. 'It's fine. So it was orphanages and the army. . . well at least you haven't any fucking relatives to bother you!'

Vic relaxed a little. 'Will the other boxers ever see these forms Harry? I just wish they hadn't written all that on my birth certificate. . . I've had to put up with some stick over the years.'

Harry finished writing and pushed the forms across the desk. 'Just sign where I've marked it. I'll get you a copy of the boxer/manager contract and no one else but the Board will see any of it. At least you *have* a birth certificate. With Tony it was orphanages and jail and he had nothing; we had to make it all up. Your clearance should be with us within a week then I'll get you some work as it looks like a busy season ahead. It's a good move on your part to turn pro; Tommy said he saw you fight in the championships and you were on the end of a bad decision. In my view you've been overlooked for the national team. The amateur game is overloaded at the top with dead wood; just look at the last Olympics, claimed there was no room for the young Spinks kid, who was working as a dustman. . . said he was too 'inexperienced' even after he'd won the national title. They only took him in the end because of newspaper pressure and he won the fucking Gold!'

Vic smiled and got up to go then looked thoughtful. 'I was quite friendly with Billy Stone. . . he watched me fight in the final and I was at his title fight win. He told me about you and Tommy and how you'd looked after him. That's why I'm here.'

Harry looked momentarily stunned at the mention of Billy's name but quickly recovered and rose to his feet. He murmered, 'Well, if you turn out as good as Billy everyone will be happy. Especially Tommy, who, by the way, is waiting for you in the gym. Good luck!'

§

A loud knock on his office door gave Harry a start and he dragged himself from deep meditation. It was Visage, Joe Hardy's odd job man.

'Come on in Visage, old pal, and sit down. You look all in, what can I do for you?'

Visage slowly walked to the bench, sat down and gazed at Harry. 'I am to give you this letter Mr Keys, from Mr Hardy about the boxing show. I had to catch the bus then walk as my bike has been stolen.'

Poor Visage had been born with a deformed face and the story had gone around that his mother had been frightened by a pig while pregnant. He'd been the butt of jokes at school which prompted his teacher, a rather pompous but well meaning man, to tell the class that in future no one was to make fun of Cyril King's visage. This of course was the worst words he could have uttered as Cyril became 'Visage' from that day forth. Joe Hardy's father, also Joe, had taken him in some years before the war giving him light work around the Granby Hotel when his ageing parents could no longer look after him. A strong rumour persists that Old Joe was the father of Cyril as he had an eye for the ladies and was known in his youth a 'bit of a lad.' If he hadn't decided to look after him, Visage might have ended up in a special home or been hidden away in an attic as so many were in those days. He had a very placid nature which belied his appearance and this was just as well for the sight of him throwing a tantrum would clear any place. Tommy always joked with him saying that if he ever left the hotel he could charge an hourly rate for haunting houses. Visage smiled and plodded on. Joe had confided in Harry one evening after a day's drinking session that his dad had stipulated in his will that the hotel was not to be sold as long as Cyril was alive and that he could live out his life there. Many times Joe would have liked to off load the place as it was nothing but hard work and Harry and Vonnie had shown an interest, but the covenant prevented him doing so and the way things were going and the state of his health, Visage would probably out live him.

Just then Fatal's head appeared around the office door. 'Hello Visage, I saw you disappear up the stairs and you looked all hot and bothered so here's a glass of lemonade for you. It's no use me offering Harry pop!' Quickly entering the office he handed the large glass to Cyril and with a nod to Harry he was gone.

Harry opened the letter and saw that everything to do with the show was neatly typed out; the names of the boxers available as opponents; wages; expenses; weigh-in times. . . all relevant detail meticulously listed. This was Joe to a tee, probably one of the best promoters in the country but lacking ambition; he would always be a big fish in a small pond.

'That's all in order Visage,' said Harry as he pressed two half crowns into his huge hand. 'So you'd best get back. . . the hotel will grind to a halt without you. I'll ring Joe and in the meantime. You make sure you get yourself a sandwich on your way home.'

Cyril got up and walked slowly to the door and turning to look Harry straight in the face he said quietly. 'I like coming here Mr Keys. I wish I could have been a boxer.'

Harry lent back in his chair, with thoughts racing through his mind. He liked Visage, but more than that he respected him for his courage in facing life and new people every day. He wished he could behave half as well. And what a great chap Joe Hardy was for looking after him. Even Fatal could occasionally let slip an act of kindness.

'Well,' thought Harry, 'in some small way these decent people and their good deeds help to even the score against all the fucking slimeball bastards in the world.'

§

With Joe Hardy's promotion coming up at the end of the week the boys were on their best behaviour as they all needed an outing and they all needed the money. The Globe reporter Adrian Close turned up with a photographer and all went well with a separate snap of Vic, Harry and Tommy and confirmation that the story would appear a few days before the show. Vic gave a brief account of his background and amateur career and his reasons for choosing this gym. He was now on the bill with Harry supplying all five fighters for one corner. It was good for business and made life better for Joe Hardy as he did his own match making and only had to find opponents.

Tommy had been spending some time on Vic getting him as fit as possible. The rest were all six round fighters and in good enough shape for that. Harry's corner was known as the 'losers area' but that didn't bother him nor his boxers for that matter. More important was lasting the distance; and the money. . . always the money. They'd already worked out how much they would walk away with after Harry totted up their subs in his little black book. They rarely asked who they were in with until the day of the fight; sometimes on these dinner shows late replacements came in as withdrawals were commonplace.

Only Vic asked who he had and just nodded when a name was mentioned, not a word about his pay.

'Joe's got a sell out again Tom! Three hundred piss-heads hissing and hollering!' shouted Harry from the office. 'And the same couple of old boilers from Staunton are the *exotic dancers* again. No comic this time, though, after the punch up with the cheeky punter.'
   Tommy strolled across to the office and lent against the door post. 'I'm pleased for Joe, Harry, he's a good guy. The punters will be blotto by the time the tinsel and tits arrive but at least a few of them will be checking Vic out.'
   Harry smiled. As usual Tom was right. Joe's four promotions a year in his hotel were good money, and an easy night's work.

§

Harry eyed Brett across his desk top, took a deep breath and opened his little black book. 'You're in to me for a nice few quid and the cash for your fight at the weekend wouldn't clear it if you walked away with nothing. Look, I can give you some work driving one of my taxis on the night shift. . . Willie's old lady is playing up again and I have to fit him in for some day work. Cash in your hand with a bit through the books. How's that sound?'
   Brett looked relieved and lent forward in his chair. 'Thanks boss, that's ideal. I can start tonight if you want me!'

'Well it will get you out of trouble for a while. Be outside here at nine o'clock and we'll give it a go. I'll explain the telephone routine then, but no picking up your fucking mates for buck-shee rides!'

'Don't worry, I'll play it straight. Any chance of a couple of quid to tide me over?'

Harry smiled and growled. 'You are a real fucking Paddy, and no mistake!' He pushed two pound notes across the desk, 'I'll see you tonight and don't be late. Time is money with taxis.'

Brett headed across the landing and into the gym. He was relieved that Harry had something for him; his gardening business had folded with bad debts sinking him but he was determined to give it another try later on.

§

Tommy was in an aggressive mood and arguing with Dicky about the punching power of an old fighter.

'And what do *you* fucking know about him? Did he ever hit you?' he bellowed. 'If his right hand missed, the draft from it would've given you fucking pneumonia! I can train you lot how to punch, but I can't make you a one-shot take-'em-out big hitter. . . they are born that way.'

He turned away out of breath from a laughing Dicky and spotted Sam at the sink, holding his hand under the cold water tap and strode across to him.

'What the fuck have you been doing outside of the gym?' he snarled, grabbing his arm. 'You didn't pick this lump up in here!'

Sam pulled away from Tommy's grip and gave his hand a kiss, 'I did a bit of demolition work and must have strained something, I'll be okay for Friday.'

'I'm the one who makes that decision,' growled Tommy. 'In the meantime don't do anything to worsen that hand; no sparring or bag work. And behave your fucking self.'

§

'What's up with Sam, Tom? No problems for Friday I hope.' queried Harry, looking concerned as he entered the gym.

'No he'll be okay. He's in with one of Tiny Ward's boxers and you know Tiny: the bravest fucking manager in the business. His kid's a real runner so Joe will get six rounds out of this one.'

Harry grinned and looked relieved. With five boxers on the bill it was a good pay day and a chance to straighten out his finances; but somehow he felt it wouldn't work out quite like that.

§

'I hope Joe's got my table near the ring Harry. My punter's like it there!' shouted Fatal as Harry and Tommy entered the crowded bar.

'He always looks after you Albert, you know that,' Harry replied. 'Just give us a couple of pints.'

Tommy leaned towards Harry and whispered. 'His fucking punters: Coupon, Billy Cox, that crooning coon layabout who's knocking off Doríce, and those scrap-metal dealers who are drunk before the meal's finished. What a fucking gang.'

Tommy was more aggressive than usual having been questioned by the local police over an incident at the Stardust Club where he worked part time on the door.

'Leave it out Tom. We get away with murder here; I owe Fatal some rent as well as money for the paint job he did on the gym.' Harry pushed across a pound note and took a sip of his drink.

'Paint job on the gym? You mean the fucking gym floor,' hissed Tom. 'I caught Eric trembling with a brush in his hand helping that lunatic Bobby Smith. There's foot prints all over the fucking place.'

'Alright, alright,' interrupted Harry, hoping to stop Tommy turning his grievances into a rant. 'Keep your voice down. Anyway, what did the law want you for?'

Tommy took a deep breath. 'Not much really. Eddie, the owner of the club, let's the brass in during week nights when the cabaret is on. Once the girls leave with a punter they can't come back in. But the Old Bill reckon they saw a few come in and out several times last week on a night when we had a crowd in.' Tommy looked around, before continuing. 'The local law know the form but there's a new guy; a fucking red haired, know-it-all Jock bastard always going on about Bannockburn - the only fucking battle they ever won - who's decided he's clamping down on everything. The usual plain clothes boys are fine; I made a statement and they'll square it all but meanwhile we have to be careful until the new bastard's off the scene.'

'Well,' muttered Harry, 'you've got to expect it. . . new broom sweeps clean and all that bollocks. He'll soon get the message.'

With a heavy sigh Tommy calmed down and looking across the bar spotted Big Gladys holding Eric by the scruff of his neck and this made him smile. 'That could only happen in this fucking mad house, give us a couple of whiskys Fatal and watch out, here comes Doríce!'

§

'He's back and he's looking good!' chorused Micky and Tony as a smiling Chalky entered the gym and headed for his locker.

'And where the fuck have you been this last couple of weeks? Back in the fucking jungle?' Chalky laughed as he expected the usual abuse. He liked it, and he liked Tommy, and would have been disappointed if nothing had been said.

'Well Mr Hardy has turned his nose up at coloured gentlemen and doesn't want any Gypsies on his bill so I indulged and took myself a sabbatical. Rest, relaxation, and contemplation, during which I carefully considered my future.' His vocal impression of an up-market Englishman, his particular party piece, set all the boxers tumbling about and Tommy couldn't keep a straight face.

'I don't need Micky's crystal ball to tell me your past or your future. Off the boat you came from bongo-bongo land with a label around your neck and your arse hanging out of your trousers, straight onto the fucking dole. And as soon as there's some work about you're like the Scarlett fucking Pimpernell. Is it too much to ask that you just keep fit and out of fucking trouble?'

Tom turned away out of breath but still smiling; then stopped in his tracks as Vic appeared to more hoots from everyone.

'And where the fuck have you been?'

Vic looked startled and turned to face him. 'I left an urgent message for you with Fatal, I had to suddenly clear out of Coupon's flat. He needed it quicky having been slung out by the widow he was with for selling off her paintings. I've moved in with Rita. . . . you know she has her own house? Fatal must have forgotten to give you the message.'

Tommy's face dropped as he contemplated what had been said. 'So it's a *fine romance* now is it? You're a quick fucking mover out of the ring, I must say. . . well, don't let none of this interfere with boxing; and never, ever leave any important messages with Fatal, he's fucking useless. Right, let's get on with training. We have a show on Friday.'

It had been rumoured that Rita had copped a house from a sugar daddy she was carrying on with after his wife found out and put a stop to it. Her benefactor was big in war surplus and she started work for his firm in the main depot where he quickly spotted her and that was the beginning of their relationship. He'd been in line for an award in the Honours List; even tipped to stand as an MP in the next election, but all that went out of the window along with Rita.

Still a very young woman, and now out of work, she'd applied for a job at the pub after being told staff were needed through a committee member friend of Doríce. Tommy had given her a long hard look after their initial 'hello' and liked what he saw. The news that Vic had moved in with her caused in him an inexplicable conflict of emotions; part of him denied he'd even been attracted to the girl, and thought the notion ridiculous, but part of him believed that when their eyes had first met, when she was being introduced by Fatal, that he'd recognised a spark of mutual attraction. The cynicism instilled in him on the battlefields of Normandy told him not to be such a gullible fool.

§

Tommy saw a great future for Vic. He'd spotted something that put the lad apart from the other boxers in the gym. Not a burning ambition for success, no hopers have that and fall by the wayside, but this Vic was gifted with that indefinable quality that he'd seen only a few times in his life: Billy Stone had it. Yet so often it disappears when women, booze, or vanity take over; or just the events of life.

'Hit that bag like you mean it, Jake.' shouted Tommy. 'It won't hit you back, and don't stand there like a fucking cigar store Indian. Move around, boxing is supposed to be the art of self defence. That's a fucking joke with you lot. Anyway, I need to check your weights when we finish tonight. I don't want any hassle later on.'

His shouting brought Harry to the gym door. 'Full house Tom. Things are looking up!'

§

'Here he comes, the fucking art expert! Buy with confidence!' bellowed a drunken Fatal as Coupon walked into the bar. It was six o'clock and Albert had been drinking all day, behind closed doors after the lunchtime session, with a bunch of costermongers from the early morning street market who'd now staggered off elsewhere.

'Good evening Albert. I gather by your welcome you've heard of the unfortunate misunderstanding involving Hyacinth's canvases.'

'*Misunder-fucking-standing*? Nine gaps on her wall and every painting up for sale at Uncle Rudy's emporium! And you with your arm up your back on the way to the nick?'

'Mr Rudelsheim failed to understand my clear instructions for a valuation only,' replied Coupon quietly. 'The gentlemen of the law have fully accepted my explanation which has the backing of Mr Rudelsheim's medical history. His mental torment caused by the prospect of a German invasion early in the war causes an occasional lapse of judgement. My course of action was due to the influx of dodgy door knockers in the area all looking for antiques and the opportunity to take advantage of the elderly.'

'Mental torment in the fucking war? The slippery bastard made a fortune on the black market. And eighty-three year old Hyacinth certainly never accepted your fucking explanation. She dumped your gear out on the front garden, misunderstanding or not and out the door you fucking went!'

Coupon, unmoved by Fatal's drunken tirade settled himself on a bar stool. 'Yes, it's true I've moved back into my apartment but I have to insist that I was not arrested but merely volunteered to help the police with their inquiries. Now a glass of your best beer, please Albert.'

Just then Doríce swept into the bar giving Fatal a withering look although there was a smile for Coupon.

'So pleased you sorted out your little problem Stanley. Hyacinth had so much trouble, war-time, with her husband. He registered as a conscientious objector, you know, and was later sent to prison for profiteering. You may have known him?'

'Known him!' screamed Fatal as he poured himself a whisky, 'He taught him fucking everything!'

Coupon hid a smile as a raging Doríce turned on Fatal. 'I suggest you retire upstairs out of my sight and out of the sight of our customers. You're a drunken disgrace. I shall watch the bar until Gladys arrives.'

Fatal lifted his glass in a mock salute to Coupon and stumbled off through the back of the bar.

'Well,' muttered Doríce, not a very good start to the evening, I think I shall have a drink and I'll put one in the till for you Stanley,'

'Many thanks Doríce.' he replied happily. 'Little setbacks are sent to try us.'

§

Harry pulled up outside the Granby Hotel, turned off the engine, let out a deep sigh and sank into thought. 'I don't seem to have got anywhere since Billy died. . . it's all happening again I've been here before.

Fuck all this déjà vu nonsense. It's my brain playing tricks on me. Maybe I should just sit quietly and gather my wits.'

Sudden shouting and swearing from the back of the van made him jump. 'Get us out of here Harry for fuck's sake! This Paddy is belching and farting. You should have sat him on the fucking roof.'

The last two words were muffled as Brett put his hand playfully across Dicky's mouth, shouting. 'Best tell him now boss that you've put him in with a gorilla tonight. That'll shut him up!'

Harry laughed as he unlocked the rear doors and out piled the four boxers Sam, Dicky, Brett and Jake.

'I swear Brett's been on the Irish stew Boss, it smells like a slaughterhouse in there.'

§

Vic was coming along in a short while as he'd been moving his bits and pieces from storage into Rita's house. Tommy was attending another interview with the police over the prostitution business at the Stardust club, and when that was over he would drive Harry's other taxi and leave it at the hotel for Brett to take after his fight. It was arranged for him to box first so he could then get to work as there was lucrative business ferrying the punters on to somewhere else or home from the hotel.

Joe was at the door to greet Harry and the boys with a smartly dress-suited Visage by his side, who all the boxers playfully attacked, much to his enjoyment.

'One down?' Joe quizzed, having made a quick count.

'No panic Joe. Vic and Tom will be here in plenty of time, everybody else here?'

'Yes,' replied Joe, now beaming and evidently relieved. 'There's a new Board inspector here but he seems okay.'

With that they all trouped inside having piled Visage up with all their bags and kidded him he would have to fight if anyone pulled out. The foyer was a rather splendid relic of a bygone era but it was downhill all the way after that.

The hotel had been used as a hospital for the wounded during the second world war and the miserly sum of money given to Joe as compensation failed to get the place back to its former glory. Joe's family had owned it since it was built in the nineteen twenties and he'd collected a very run down shell on his return from the far east where he'd been a prisoner of the 'little yellow monkeys,' - a term he always used to describe the Japs. Joe had never recovered his health after that ordeal. He'd tried his best since but it was hard going. The boxing shows put a few quid in his pocket.

Visage dumped the boxer's bags in the home changing room and they all wandered into the main hall. No punters there yet and it looked very smart with all tables neatly laid out with the ring in the centre. Six hours later it would look like a bomb had hit it.

'We may as well do the weigh-in now and get it out the way.' said Harry to the Board inspector, who had been looking intently into the pond Joe had near the entrance. 'Vic Lane can be checked later if that's okay?'

'Yes that's fine Mr Keys,' he replied. 'I'll attend to that right away,' and they all proceeded down the hallway to the general office now deputising as the weighing-in room. Nearing the entrance the Inspector turned to Joe and asked in a friendly manner. 'Are there any fish in your aquatic feature gracing the foyer, Mr Hardy?'

'No sir,' replied Joe sadly. 'Not any more, the cat had 'em all.'

8

Brett went on first and was obviously in with a no-hoper who was looking for somewhere to lie down as soon as the bell rang. They went through the motions for two rounds then after a minute of the third amid hoots and howls of derision, down he went from a punch no-one else saw and was counted out. He livened up on his way back to the dressing room when a boozy punter called him a few names. Brett dived in between them and pushed him out of harm's way.

Tommy had just arrived having missed the bout but the corner was taken care of by the house seconds.

Vic looked relaxed if a little tired from moving all his things to Rita's house.

'You're on now Dicky and give us six rounds. Are you okay Brett?'

'Yeah Tom I'm fine, I'll have him again anytime, tell Harry I've gone off to work now.'

'Will do, well done and take it steady, you look headed for a busy night.' replied a unusually happy Tommy as he felt relaxed with everyone on site. 'Jake you go after Dicky and then it's the interval leaving Sam and Vic to follow.'

Just then Harry walked in obviously having had a few drinks in the small bar across the road. 'I just looked in the dining room - it's packed solid. Great for Joe, but where's Brett?'

'He's already been on, won in three, and is now out grafting for you,' shouted Tom. 'I want Vic to go on last, his kid is a tough nut so should be there at the end. It will give us a chance to see how he's coming on. A good first outing for him.'

'Yeah, fine,' slurred a slightly swaying Harry, as he headed in towards the bar.

Dicky boxed to instructions and Tom was pleased as the rounds went by with the win never in doubt. Jake was his usual flashy self which the customers liked; mistaking it for superior ability which he did not have. He knew his opponent having boxed him three times before and the moves they made could almost have been choreographed, but it looked good. This time he lost the decision and feigned disbelief running to the four corners of the ring pleading to the punters; most of whom had betted on his corner. It all went down well and took the show to the interval.

Suddenly Joe, looking distraught, appeared in the dressing room. 'Tommy, here quick!' he spluttered, grabbing his shirt sleeve and pulling him away from cutting off Jake's bandages. 'Where's Harry?'

Just then a smiling Harry appeared but stopped short when he saw Joe. 'So far so good. What's the long face for?'

'There's been a terrible accident,' gasped Joe. 'Your depot man just rang. It's Brett, he's been in a crash and he's dead.'

Harry slumped back against the wall, a look of total shock and disbelief crossed his face. 'What? What. . . when did Fred ring? Are you sure it's not a hoax? Some dopey bastard trying to wreck things?'

'No Harry. Fred put me onto the law; they were stood with him in the office. They got the depot address from inside the taxi. There's no doubt about it; you must ring them straight away. I'm so sorry.'

Harry reached for the piece of paper in Joe's outstretched hand. Tom said nothing, his arms hanging down by his side like a puppet whose strings had been cut. The boxers were silent and motionless.

Harry took a deep breath. 'Don't say anything to anybody about this tonight Joe. Drag out the interval until I get my head together. I'll go and find out what happened.'

§

Harry often had flashbacks to the war, being called to investigate a device which almost always turned out to be an unexploded bomb. He had that same feeling of dread that he would not be able to cope with the situation. The Billy Stone business had shattered him and he'd never fully recovered. Now Brett. He followed Joe into his office and picked up the telephone. Joe grabbed the piece of paper from Harry and read out the number as he dialled. A matter-of-fact voice answered.

'Whitton police station, Constable Verry speaking.'

'This is Harry Keys, I have been asked to ring you regarding a traffic accident involving Brett Doyle.'

'Yes Mr Keys, perhaps it would be better if you came into the station as soon as possible. It's not appropriate to discuss the matter over the telephone.'

Harry took a deep breath and in a cold and calculating voice which made Joe stand up with a look of horror on his face said, 'Never mind all that appropriate bollocks. Is my boxer dead, or what?'

The line went quiet except for some muffled mumblings before a different voice said hesitantly. 'Yes Mr Keys there has been a fatality. I understand from Mr Hardy you have a boxing show tonight so please call in at your earliest convenience and ask for Inspector Allen. I am very sorry to give you this sad news.'

Harry put the receiver back without replying. 'Fucking hell Joe, what next?'

§

Sam went on after the interval and ground out a decision which nobody commented upon as by then most of the punters were drunk. Tommy did the corner and for once refrained from his usual cross talk and banter with Fatal and his gang who were shouting their comments with increasing volume from their table as the drink went down. Vic was more subdued than ever and entered the ring completely ignoring the shouts from punters who'd read Adrian Stone's piece on him in the local paper. The genuine boxing followers had waited for this fight.

He boxed carefully for four rounds taking no chances but without giving his previous unstoppable opponent any real trouble. Then suddenly in the fifth he cut loose with a left right combination that made even the most drunken punter gasp. Tommy, watching with an incredulous look on his face, felt slightly frightened as his game opponent slumped to the canvas. The count was a formality and as Vic walked back to his corner it was impossible not to see a ruthless smile crease his ashen face as he muttered. 'That was for Brett!'

§

Willie, Harry's other taxi driver picked him up after the show and took him to Vonnie's house. He'd given her the news and she felt it would be better if he stayed there and not go back to Fatal's for an all night booze up. Tommy went back to the pub but the boxers went their separate ways. Chalky, Johnny, and Micky who hadn't boxed were already there and had heard the news and gave Tom a hug and mumbled commiserations when he reached their corner of the bar.

It was a subdued gathering with a strangely sober Fatal and for once a contrite Doríce behind the bar helping Big Gladys and Eric. Tommy felt a hand on his shoulder followed by Coupon's unmistakable voice.

'So sorry about Brett, just when things were picking up, but hey Tom, this Vic looks the part!'

He turned slowly and looked straight at him, reaching for a drink Fatal had put in front of him. 'Thanks Coup, thanks, but it's early days with Vic, let's hope so, we shall see.'

§

Harry called at the police station early next morning, Vonnie having dropped him off on her way into Whitton where she work in a solicitor's office. Inspector Allen gave him very little information on what had happened. No other vehicle was involved, the taxi had left the road at Bents Corner near where Billy Stone had died, went down the embankment and crashed into a tree. The ambulance crew found Brett slumped over the wheel dead. No reason could be given yet for the accident and the post mortem results will not be known for a few days. The Inspector added that the local newspaper had already been making inquiries about the tragedy.

He left still in a shocked state and walked the mile or so to Fatal's. It was closed so he went in through the back door and into the bar where Eric was cleaning up .

'Hi Harry,' he chirped then changed his tone as he suddenly remembered what had happened the night before. 'Terrible Harry, terrible, I'm glad I don't drive, I liked him he was always nice to me.'

Harry gave him a smile. 'Thanks Eric, did everyone behave last night?'

'Yes Harry, yes, only a few boxers were in, they'd heard about Brett. Rita had the night off so it was me and Gladys until Mr Cort got back with his gang then Mrs Cort came down to help. Tommy got drunk and was shouting but didn't cause any trouble and nobody stayed very late.'

Just then Fatal appeared in the doorway, he was half-dressed and looked a mess. 'I heard voices so I came to investigate as Eric is apt to let anybody in who looks half decent.'

Eric turned away and went on with his tidying up.

'What a giant fuck-up Harry, just when all is going well again. Any idea what happened?'

Harry let out a sigh and lent on the bar. 'Not really, he left the road and crashed into a tree, they're doing all the usual tests on the motor and we'll know more in a few days. Give us a large scotch Albert, it's been a long morning.'

He was well drunk by the time the boxers began arriving at the gym around mid day for the usual post mortem on their fights and a general loosening up but nothing too strenuous, then it was downstairs into the bar. Tommy followed them in and they all congregated in their corner. The pub was strangely quiet for the day following a show as usually everyone liked to voice their opinion on what they thought about the night before Fatal had smartened himself up and Doríce had appeared shedding a tear as she hugged Harry and Tommy which made them flinch.

Turning to Tommy who was still drunk from the night before Harry mumbled. 'The press have already been asking questions about what happened to Brett; Fatal's had phone calls and told them he doesn't know anything.'

All conversation stopped as Tommy's glass crashed down on the bar spilling what was left of his beer and spreading his arms in an old fashioned fighting pose he shouted. 'As sure as my name is Tommy Law if that fucking son-of-a-bitch faggot reporter says anything to me I'll break his fucking jaw.'

Harry shuddered and everyone nearby was shocked and looked away. 'Hold on Tom. Hold on,' he soothed. 'Take it easy, we all know he's a wrong 'un but he's all there is locally and we don't want to lose him.'

This seemed to steady Tommy down and he looked glumly at his empty glass. 'Okay, okay, that's it, I don't want to do anything to hurt the gym. Give us another pint Fatal and don't look so fucking worried!'

§

Harry had never been a man who reflected much on his past life. Sometimes he thought about the might-have-beens, the missed opportunities and the disasters. He certainly would not have remembered much about the week following Brett's death as he stayed at Vonnie's place with a supply of whisky until one night he got roaring drunk and she sent him away in his own remaining taxi.

Tommy was boozed up most of the time and completely unapproachable. The pub was busier than usual with everyone talking about the accident and what caused it. It brought back vivid memories of the Billy Stone tragedy still fresh in everyone's mind.

Fatal managed to say the wrong thing as usual. When surveying his packed pub he voiced the opinion that it was an 'ill wind that did nobody any good' which prompted Tommy to threaten to punch his fat face in. Even Doríce looked shocked and tore into him shouting so all could hear. 'Albert, how dare you say a thing like that, apologise to Tom and the boys immediately.'

He looked exactly what he was, a bloated, drunken bag of wind and her withering attack, whether genuine or not, stopped him in his tracks. 'Sorry Tom, sorry boys, you all know I didn't mean anything by it.'

They all turned away and looked towards the door as Harry staggered in, obviously the worse for wear. Tommy steadied him as he reached their corner and shouted for a drink which Fatal fetched with an unusual turn of speed.

'No booze involved in Brett's accident,' Harry said for all to hear. 'I've just had the report, they can't say what happened, all sorts of rumours: fell asleep; going too fast; all that bollocks; but the speedo was on nil and the police mechanics said the car was sound so I suppose. . . we'll never know.'

He took a long drink from his pint and turning back to Tommy growled out. 'I've arranged the funeral for eleven next Monday morning at the local church and the undertaker has fixed a plot. The police have contacted a brother up country somewhere who said he'll attend, seems there's nobody else. I don't suppose there's any fucking money anywhere so I shall cop for the bill. What's more, my taxi is a fucking write off.'

Meanwhile everyone just went through the motions, biding time until Brett's funeral was out of the way. All the active boxers were in the gym, training, but with little enthusiasm and very subdued. Even Tommy was quiet and there was no verbal sparring with anyone. The pub was busy with Fatal and Doríce adopting a sad expression whenever Brett's name was mentioned; nevertheless they were genuinely upset, especially Doríce, who seemed to have had a soft spot for him as he was always friendly and better behaved that the rest of the boxers.

Vic and Rita seemed to be very much involved with each other and she was a good bar maid which was just as well as she and Big Gladys kept the place going when Fatal got drunk and Doríce went missing. Then there was always Eric to tidy up and he hadn't had a funny turn for a while.

Harry spent most of the week at Vonnie's house, keeping out of the pub and off the booze although he knew it wouldn't last.

§

At the weekend two characters turned up at the pub, both with strong Irish accents claiming to be Brett's brothers. They showed Fatal and Doríce a letter from the local police addressed to Dermot Doyle informing him of his brother's death and asking him to contact the police station at his earliest convenience. Although they were both smartly dressed they had no apparent luggage apart from one large carrier bag and it looked like they had just come out of prison as they sported that pallor prisoner's get in there from not enough fresh air and exercise.

Straight into the bar on Saturday night, they seemed in no hurry to leave with no obvious money problems. There was the usual palaver at closing time with drunken customers and the two of them could not remember where they were staying so Doríce let them get their heads down in the lounge with a blanket slung over them and they were propping up the bar again at opening time next morning after a short walk around the block.

Letters, cards and telephone calls arrived at the pub expressing sadness and regret at Brett's death from promoters, managers and boxers but that was the way it was and had been when Billy was killed. Doríce kept a careful note of the calls and passed all the correspondence on to Harry. He met up with Tom and the boxers in the bar on Sunday lunchtime to go over the arrangements for the funeral next day.

'Get tomorrow over with Tom then try and get back to normal, there's plenty of work and we need to keep Vic active as he seems to be the only one who might be going somewhere.'

Tommy put his drink down and looked wistfully at the large photograph of Billy behind the bar. 'Vic is better than Billy was at this stage; I think he'll go all the way.'

Harry leant heavily on the bar and thought for a few seconds before answering. 'Then he must be good, only time will tell. . . Blimey! Look at those Paddys! What sort of fucking state are they going to be in tomorrow?'

Tommy started to smile as he gazed across the bar room at them. 'They're good guys Harry and not half as bad as they look. I spent some time with them last night; you should have a chat. . . they'd like to talk to you.'

Harry let out a long sigh and looked across at them again. 'Yeah, I know what you mean but now doesn't seem the right moment with so much happening. After the funeral we will all get together.'

§

Fatal with his usual eye to business - prompted no doubt by Doríce - opened the pub for pre-funeral drinks at nine o'clock on Monday morning. The two Paddys were the first customers in, as they'd again spent the previous night in the pub lounge.

'Doríce!' he shouted as the two of them emerged dishevelled through the bar room door. Doríce appeared behind the bar dressed like she was going to the races rather than a funeral and a look of horror crossed her face when she gave her lodgers a glance.

'Albert! Albert. . . it would be more appropriate if our customers were offered a cup of tea at this moment. They have a busy morning ahead!'

Fatal paused, his right hand half-reaching for the whisky bottle. 'Of course Doríce, exactly what I was thinking. . . right away.'

The pained expression which appeared on Dermot's face said it all. Con was too far gone to have grasped the conversation.

'And Albert, make sure at ten thirty that everyone is ready to leave. Harry's taxi is ferrying people to the church and I don't want any problems with stragglers. Is this understood?'

'Yes Doríce, understood, all will be well.'

Willie, who was driving Harry's remaining taxi, collected him and Vonnie from her house and they arrived at the church early. Harry wanted to make sure everyone behaved as there'd been a punch up at Billy's funeral between rival factions. Tommy was the first of the boxing crowd on site and stood talking to Harry while Vonnie stood a little distance away reading the path-side gravestones.

Harry surveyed the surroundings feeling sad at the turn of events and apprehensive for the future. 'We'd best vet all the boys as they arrive, Tom, as the vicar's a funny old bastard at the best of times. After the performance at Billy's funeral he'll stop the service and call the police if trouble looms.'

Tommy nodded and smiled as he spotted some of the boxers coming through the archway gate. 'What the fuck's Micky got on? A clown's suit?'

Harry swung around and let out a gasp of astonishment as the group approached, blurting out. 'Christ Mick what have you come as?'

They all stopped a few yards away and Micky, stretching out his arms in a theatrical gesture, exclaimed in an affected voice. 'I am celebrating Brett's *life*; not his *death* and we should all do the same. Right, boys?'

Harry saw a crowd of grinning faces and for once was lost for words.

He was brought back to reality with the arrival of Dermot and Con. 'Just look at the state of these two. . . get after them Tom for fuck's sake, they're going the wrong way!'

Suddenly there was Fatal wedged into his black suit, gold watch and chain looped across his fat gut, stumbling along arm in arm with Dorice who was wearing what looked like a sombrero. Behind them sauntered a smug, smiling white suited Erwin and behind him Coupon, sporting a suitable hang-dog expression and looking the part in his pre-war pin stripe. Harry felt like giving up and letting everything run its course when Vonnie suddenly elbowed him in the ribs and pointed excitedly to Big Gladys, Rita, and Vic. 'Is that Eric with them, what *have* they dressed him up in?'

Tommy burst out laughing as Eric passed by in what could only be described as jodhpurs and a straight jacket.

'Oh my heaven!' exclaimed Harry, grabbing Vonnie's arm. 'They must think he's due for a turn. Let's get inside before the newspaper crowd arrive or Tom will end up punching somebody. Come on, we'll grab a pew at the back ready for a quick getaway!'

The solitary hearse slowly approached the church door. There were no mourners' cars but quite a crowd of boxing followers had turned up and lined the pathway. Eric narrowly avoided being run over as he darted out, Big Gladys grabbing him just in time. The undertaker and his assistants carried the coffin into the church, down the aisle and onto some trestles. Harry thought how small the coffin looked, shiny wood with just a bunch of flowers on top in the shape of a boxing glove.

Strange thoughts sped through his head, as the church filled up from the back rows towards the front. Teddy Long, Sid Suthall and Joe Hardy along with a very smartly dressed Visage were the only ones who went to the front pew. It was if everyone wanted to distance themselves from Brett or what remained of him.

The vicar visibly shuddered when he spotted Micky and the gang but stumbled up the steps to the pulpit. Vonnie squeezed Harry's arm as Doríce's sobs began to be heard above the wailing organ music and gave him a knowing look. The vicar went on about 'gone to a better place' and all that bollocks, which at twenty two years of age Brett would not have wanted to hear. This was followed with a brief mention of boxing and a thank you to all who are in attendance, a reminder of the collecting plates at the end of each pew, and the wake to follow at the Cricketers Arms.

The organist seemed to be two bars behind the singers, and coming to the crescendo in The Old Rugged Cross it proved too much for Eric who had been singing heartily and he started to wobble about but again Big Gladys came to the rescue with an arm lock. Then Con the Paddy rushed out glazed-eyed and threw up outside the vestry door making so much noise that the vicar stopped delivering his final remarks on Brett's short life and asked one of the undertaker's assistants to investigate. The young man returned ashen faced after being told loudly to fuck off. Then it was all over. The coffin was carried out and balanced on trestles by a dug-out hole. A few more words from the vicar and down Brett went.

Harry stood looking at the scene as if it was all mistake, a nightmare, but the sudden presence of the undertaker brought him back to reality. He held his breath, expecting details of the bill and when it would be paid.

'A very sad day Mr Keys, please accept our heartfelt condolences,' he muttered, looking like something out of a horror film. Moving even closer he continued. 'Mr Doyle requested the funeral account, including costs for the grave stone which will be put in place in due course and has left details of the inscription. This has all been paid for in advance, a most unusual occurrence nowadays don't you think? Good day, Mr Keys!'

And with a knowing look he walked off down the path.

Words failed Harry, and he just mumbled. 'Thank you.' After all the fuss over Billy's funeral costs which almost went to court this was a shock.

It was Dermot who approached him next.

'Brett always had good words for you Mr Keys. If he left anything of value please give it to the local workhouse. I haven't checked his rooms and we're off soon. Do you know if he had any debts?'

Harry shook his outstretched hand then took a step back from the blast of booze fumes. These were the first words they had spoken and he was suddenly ashamed of the way he had avoided the two of them. He knew Brett was in the book for a few quid but be that as it may.

'None that I am aware of Dermot. I would have heard by now if there was any.'

'Thank you then Mr Keys and goodbye. We'll be on our way now.'

With that he beckoned to Con and they walked slowly to the church gate and into the taxi Willie had parked there.

§

Harry overheard local reporter Adrian Stone say to a companion. 'Another Keys' boxer bites the dust,' in a stage whisper that would certainly have prompted Tommy into action if he'd heard but he was deeply engrossed in conversation with Teddy Long and Sid Suthall.

'Are you ready Harry? Everyone is going back to the pub but I must be in work this afternoon so I'll give it a miss. Perhaps it would be better if you did as well.'

73

It was Vonnie's quiet tone that made him realise it was a good idea as a chance word could set arguments going.

'Yes that will do me. We'll walk a bit until Willie gets back; let them all get on with it.'

And get on with it they did. Teddy and Sid continued their animated discussion with Tommy and his boxers in the bar and then left a five pound note with Fatal for further drinks. Jack Silver had been unable to attend the funeral but sent a flashy sympathy card and twenty quid for mourner's refreshments. The card with a mention of his generous donation was pinned up in a prominent place behind the bar. It was all Fatal, Doríce and Big Gladys could do to serve the punters and Eric minus his straight jacket was trying his best. Willie had been busy after dropping Harry at his flat and Vonnie at her office, ferrying all and sundry back to the pub.

Earlier he had left Dermot and Con at the railway station and received a thirty bob tip and was now at Harry's flat for further orders.

'They were alright, those two Harry, they really were, it was a shame they couldn't stay longer.'

Harry nodded and poured himself his second large scotch. 'Yeah, they were, but now life has to go on, you can park up the taxi and have the rest of the day off, thanks for keeping on top of things this last week.'

Willie looked pleased. 'Thanks boss, I'll see you tomorrow.'

Harry never had any problem with drinking alone, in fact he always joked he could drink in a darkened room, he liked alcohol, and the feeling it gave him. He despised those so called regular drinkers who turned up at the same time every night for their couple, never more, then off home. If you are going to drink, have a fucking drink and don't mess about. He drank when he felt like it, mostly every day, whatever the time or place, when he wanted a drink that was it, and it was it right now.

§

Harry received a phone call from Inspector Allen who requested he visit the police station at his earliest convenience for a chat and just assumed some more information had come to light about Brett's accident. He was surprised when a large file was produced which contained a photo of Brett, his two brothers, and various other men. 'What's all this about Inspector?' he asked. 'I can see Brett, Dermot, and Con but who are the others?' The Inspector lent forward in his chair and turned over some pages.

'You may have noticed the presence of some strangers in the *Cricketer's Arms* prior to Brett Doyle's funeral, Mr Keys. They were undercover police not connected to this station who were observing the movements of Dermot and Cornelius Doyle, who have convictions for illegal arms sales and smuggling. Although a brother, your boxer has never been involved, but nevertheless it had been thought necessary to monitor his activities for some considerable time and with his violent death and the arrival of his brothers, alarm bells started to ring. You will appreciate that all this procedure was completely out of my hands. I may add that your excellent war service record is also contained in this file and it convinced a higher authority at government level to brief you on what has been going on, although I can assure you that you have never been under any suspicion for irregular activity. Apart from some heavy drinking the two brothers met and talked to no strangers and the fact that they stayed in the pub enabled the police to watch them more closely. Now they have left the town the matter is closed as far as this police station is concerned. I may add that the licensee was *not* taken into our confidence, for various reasons. You are the only person with clearance to be privy to this information.'

Harry gasped for breath. 'Well Inspector I must say that I spent very little time in the pub prior to the funeral and in fact only spoke to Brett's brothers for the first time as they were leaving the church. I am shocked with all this - in Whitton of all places - and that my boxer Brett had been watched for some time.'

Inspector Allen closed the file and relaxed a little. 'Yes Mr Keys, I appreciate your shock and concern but should either of the brothers contact you in the future, for whatever reason, please inform me immediately.'

Harry nodded, stood up and shook hands. 'I will Inspector and now I need a drink!'

Harry walked slowly out of the police station and down the road towards the pub trying to take in what had been discussed. The few times he'd visited the pub before the funeral he had never noticed anything untoward although some strange faces appeared from time to time but he put that down to curiosity about the death of Brett and the newspaper stories. Now he was 'in the frame' with ongoing investigations about arms dealing. He stopped and gazed up at the clear blue sky. 'What fucking next!' he muttered.

§

There was plenty of work around for the boys and Micky won and lost, Chalky won in a great nobbins fight while Sam, Dicky, Johnny and Jake all had a bout each with only Dicky winning but they all stayed on their feet and were there at the end so that counts as a good result. Tommy seemed as preoccupied with Vic as he had been with Billy Stone but never so much with Kenny Cole. Vic had three fights winning them all inside the distance and was due out again on a Teddy Long show. Sid Suthall was doing all the matching and used Vic whenever possible. His knockout record was becoming impressive and they were not all push overs.

Harry had been absent from the gym and the pub leaving it all to Tom, just giving the various deals the nod but rarely commenting on anything else. So it was somewhat of a surprise when he entered the pub bar at around nine o'clock on the evening before Vic was fighting, heading straight for Tommy and the gang at their usual place in the far corner.

'I suppose I had better buy you lot a drink as you all seem to have been behaving yourselves and doing some work!'

Tom slapped him on the back and the boys all hooted.

'Give this lot a drink Fatal and have one yourself.'

Fatal looked up with bleary eyes and shouted a welcome while Eric, and Big Gladys gave him a wave. 'One pound two shillings then Harry, and guess what? That Charlie Coates dropped fucking dead this morning on his car lot. How about that? Gone and left all that fucking money.'

Tommy grinned and shouted. 'If I go with half a crown in my pocket it will be half a crown too fucking soon.'

Harry had to smile and the boys roared with laughter but it was Doríce who brought everyone back down to earth as she had been sitting unnoticed near them chatting to some members of the pub committee.

'Albert that is a disgraceful way to talk about Charlie who was a pillar of our local society and did so much for the under privileged. Also this foul, language must stop. . . from everyone!'

Harry winced and looked at Fatal, they all knew Doríce had a fling with Charlie in her younger days; he was a right one for the girls.

'Well Doríce we all know what he got up to and it's no wonder his heart gave out.'

This was Fatal as good as he got, answering Doríce back. Something he would never do when sober. She gave one of her theatrical flounces and continued muttering to her immediate company. The gang turned away all grinning, it looked like being a good night. Harry took a long swig from his pint. It tasted good and he felt good, he was back in the fold.

'Vic and the boys have been busy these last few weeks, Tom. I never did ask you what Teddy and Sid were on about after the funeral, best bring me up to date. . .'

Tommy beamed, looking pleased with everything; and more so on seeing Harry for longer than a few minutes, which was all the time he had spent around the gym recently. 'Well it's all good,' he said excitedly. 'They have a lot of shows with too few boxers, and of course Teddy and Sid are in with Jack Silver and television so they need us. They wanted to talk to you after the funeral but you disappeared and only this morning left a message with Fatal for you to ring Teddy as soon as you can. Vic is doing great and seems settled with Rita, for the time being anyway. He's resting tonight as he's fighting tomorrow.'

Right Tom, it all sounds to be running smoothly, I had better stay away regularly and leave it to you!'

Tommy laughed loudly and again slapped Harry on the back. 'Let's have a good drink for Charlie, he wasn't a bad old bastard.'

9

Harry wasn't sure what to do. The gym was ticking over with all the boxers busy and earning money. Vic had won two more fights inside the distance and people were beginning to notice him and ask questions. The newspapers had picked up the story and had done another piece and pen pictures of all the active boxers.

Some hilarious photographs of the *Cricketers Arms* public bar also appeared in the feature showing Fatal and Doríce done up like a couple of dogs' dinners.

Naturally the article was slanted towards the double tragedy but was tastefully done despite the muttered threats of Tommy and his still burning ambition to thump that 'fucking faggot reporter.'

Letters had also been arriving from the council intimating that developments were again planned for the area which meant pulling down all the condemned properties, clearing all the war time bomb damage which still littered the area and then building houses. This had been muted for years and Coupon was forever reading out the latest communication in the pub bar as the houses he owned nearby were marked for demolition.

Harry didn't want to suddenly have to move from his flat which was included in the plans so he thought about asking Vonnie if he could gradually move in but she was adamant that they get married or carry on as they are at present, living apart for most of the time. He figured that perhaps marriage wouldn't be so bad but shivered at the thought of what would happen when he got home after a drinking bout, which he knew was always on the cards. It was too late to change, and he didn't want to.

Any pressure from whatever direction and Harry reached for a drink; or maybe that was just an excuse as he was unable to remember a time when he did not drink. And there was Tommy who drank every day without fail and most discussions took place in Fatal's bar. How would he cope standing there drinking, with his mind half on boxing and the other half wondering what state he would be in when he finally had to go home and face Vonnie. Maybe he would take her out to Jack's restaurant and see what she had to say after showing her the council's letter.

In the meantime he had best get to Fatal's as the meeting with Teddy and Sid had been arranged for mid day in the lounge bar.

§

'In all my years in boxing there have never been better times ahead - and I mean that gents. Best forget old squabbles and move on,' said a smiling Sid Suthall as he and Teddy Long settled down in Fatal's lounge bar which was closed to customers and where they could talk without any of the bar crowd overhearing their business. Harry and Tommy had already shaken hands with them both and seemed relaxed.

'Teddy and me will be working closely with Jack Silver as you know anyway, he not only has the television contract but is also continuing with his small hall shows. But not in areas to interfere with ours, so for all your fighters it can be *have gum-shield will travel.*'

Harry lent back in his chair, he liked Sid while Teddy was a somewhat acquired taste. A bit too flash for his own good and the Kenny Cole deal still rankled although he put no blame whatever on Sid for what happened; as usual it was all about money.

'We will be able to use at least two of your fighters, perhaps more on most of the shows and we intend putting Vic as top of the bill shortly if that is agreeable to you both and the opponent is okay. . .'

Sid was about to continue when Tommy interrupted. 'That all sounds great Sid and will you both be doing the dealings with Jack when television and extra money is involved? And am I correct in saying that you, Sid, are handling all the matchings for Jack's shows?'

Sid smiled and gave a clap of his hands. 'Yes Tom myself and Teddy will get all deals down on paper then contact Harry for him to discuss it with you; especially the matchings which I will be doing for all our shows, wherever the venue might be, that way you will know who to bawl and shout at if things are not to your liking. Too many people involved only causes problems as we all know from past experience.'

Teddy spoke for the first time looking from Harry to Tommy and back again. 'Sid mentioned we would like Vic to top the bill which would be at Billingham, no television but a great venue. Vic is making a name for himself and building up a following without really putting himself about. The show is in three weeks' time so he can go out again before that but I know you will be careful. I'll get back to you with the money side and Sid will sort out an opponent and also fix up a couple more of your boys, how does that all sound?'

Tommy nodded his approval and looked across to Harry who also nodded and replied. 'We'll go along with that. What plans are there for Kenny? I read the Board stipulated he has a mandatory defence of his title due.'

He'd directed this question straight at Teddy as he was Kenny's manager who suddenly looked uncomfortable but fired back. He'd obviously expected Kenny's name to come up at sometime.

'You're right Harry, a mandatory defence of the title is due and scheduled for six weeks' time on Jack's Big Time Boxing Night with television and all the trimmings. We don't know who he's in with yet as the final eliminator is next week. It'll be really something with some of your fighters on the bill as well.'

Harry nodded again and was about to say something to Tom when Eric appeared with a shuddering tray of tea.

'Mrs Cort sent this in for you, is everything all right?'

Tommy helped him settle the tray on the narrow table and gave him a friendly swipe. 'Yes Eric all's well and please thank Mrs Cort.'

They all sipped their tea and chatted generally. It had been a convivial meeting with no harsh words and everything looked good for the immediate future.

'Well we'd better get back and start the phone calls,' said a rather tired looking Sid. 'No doubt you and Tom have plenty to do.'

Teddy pulled on his coat, shook hands with Harry and Tommy then tossed a ten bob note on the tea tray. 'For the young lad,' he said. And then they were gone.

'That all went well, Tom. Let's have one in the bar before tackling that lot upstairs!'

Tommy was looking at the crumpled note on the tea tray and grunted. 'That sounds good to me, but that fucking Teddy can't help being Mr Flash.'

§

Tommy was puzzled as to why Vic failed to complain like all the rest of the boxers, about how fights were arranged, opponents, money, expenses and just everything connected with the gym and boxing. If he had issues he kept them to himself. Even Rita said he rarely discussed boxing and his ambitions but seemed happy the way things were going and gave the impression he knew exactly where it would all end. He liked his drinks with the boys in Fatal's bar but some of them had commented that he never talked about his past or his hopes for the future. It was the now that meant everything to him and with that he seemed to be content.

It un-nerved Tommy that he was reminded so much of Billy by Vic's mannerisms, the long periods of silence, and certain areas of his boxing style. He'd noticed how he could change his mode of attack after quickly spotting an opponent's weak points very early in a bout and then deliver a vicious combination of punches to end the fight. It was as if he reached a time when he knew the fight was his and saw no need to carry on.

The crowd loved a hitter and Vic was certainly that. Teddy had been right when he said he was building up a good local following. The rest of the boxers enjoyed his success as it meant more work for them and it gave Harry more bargaining power when fight bills were arranged. They'd all had a great run along with Billy on his path to the title and his death had been a terrible blow to all of them and a massive setback for the gym. Now Brett was gone and it was pick up time all over again.

§

The Billingham show came and went with a full house and another knockout win for Vic. Chalky went the distance for a points loss and gave his usual look of amazement when the referee raised his opponent's hand. Although promoters had become reluctant to use Micky because of his volatile Gipsy following Harry made it part of the package and he did not disappoint his mob with a vintage display of box fighting causing the fight to be stopped in the third round. Tommy always knew he had talent but like so many of them for some unknown reason neglected it. Harry had watched all three fights and mingled with the Gipsy fans making sure that all was well.

A smiling Sid settled up the wages with a flourish and was obviously delighted with the evening.

'That Vic suddenly turned it on when I was beginning to think he was in some sort of trouble and did you see how he turned away when he landed that big right hand as if he knew it was all over and Tommy staring at him with a strange look on his face, no excitement at all, come on Harry what's going on?'

Harry slowly counted the money as if to give himself time to think about an answer, it had been a strange end to a fight and a particularly clinical knockout of a very capable boxer.

'I can't give away our fight plans Sid, me and Tom spend hours working things out, just you and Teddy keep the action coming in.'

Sid grinned and gave him a friendly punch as Tommy entered the office.

'A great night Sid, full house but what's that Bobby Cooke doing selling fucking programmes, he's a former champion, I think it's sad to see him doing that for a few tanners, don't you?'

Sid had an embarrassed look on his face and started to mutter a reply when Harry quickly interrupted. 'Tom,… it's always sad when you've got no fucking money.'

§

Harry was drinking, alone in his rooms. He didn't really know why he was carrying on after the usual booze up in Fatal's. He would normally stagger home or get Willie to pick him up and then fall asleep, but he wanted a drink, maybe for all the drinks he'd missed over the years when trying to behave himself. He could think of a hundred reasons why people said they drank: all that bollocks about absent friends, loneliness, the stress of life and being unable to cope with everyday things. It was really none of those with him. He liked alcohol and he liked drinking. He didn't give a fuck about being sociable, him and Tom could never be accused of that. He knew he should have curbed the boxers' drinking years ago. But how could he, when him and Tom usually kept it going?

The gym and boxing was everything to him, there was nothing else over which he had some control. Business was good with nobody arguing. He had a good stable of boxers and then there was Vic. He really didn't know what to make of him. He seemed settled with Rita who definitely knew how many beans made five and looked like she could handle him. But what puzzled him was that he didn't understand where Vic wanted to go or whether he was really good enough to go anywhere. A clean sheet so far with no defeats and rarely in any sort of trouble but Tom was strangely quiet about him after his initial statement that he was better than Billy at this stage of his career, so he left Vic to him.

Maybe that was his problem, always leaving things to someone else. To Tom, Vonnie, Sid and Teddy and now the big wheel Jack Silver. He hadn't had the courage to approach Vonnie again about moving in, maybe soon, maybe never. The more he drank the more he cursed everybody and everything, all for no logical reason.

What the fuck he thought and stood up shouting. 'I have nothing to be ashamed of! All the years in the army fighting for my country. I can walk in anywhere and somebody will always buy me a fucking drink, pubs everywhere, one on every corner. I'll do it all now before the good times are gone forever.'

He slumped back into his chair, breathless and reached for the bottle of whisky, thinking how much he really did like the stuff.

§

'Come here a minute Tom!' Harry shouted excitedly from the office. 'I've got some good news for you.' Tommy broke off his conversation with Jake and strolled through the open office door, giving Vic a friendly punch as he passed. He noticed how tidy everything looked for a change with boxers' files neatly stacked on the desk.

'Just took a call from Teddy. Kenny's got Timmy Norton for his title defence; he won the eliminator on points and Vic can go in with Eddie Soames for the Area Title, all agreed by the Board. How Jack Silver swung that I didn't ask. . . well what do you think?'

Tommy slumped down onto the long bench and leant back against the wall trying to catch his breath; but before he could answer Harry continued. 'Both fights will be on television and Teddy has asked for two of our boys for six rounders. Well, how does all that sound?'

'We're on with all of it!' Tom blurted out as Harry's obvious excitement reached him. 'We'll give Vic another bout before then - an eight rounder on the Walton show. Sid's doing the matching. Fucking hell Harry, this could be our breakthrough again!'

Getting the okay calmed down Harry and he searched through his pocket book for Teddy's number as Tom went back into the gym. The news of Vic's title fight quickly spread around the gym and down into the pub. He confirmed everything with

Teddy and a meeting was arranged to discuss the money side. Tom suggested Tony and Chris for the six rounders as they were more likely to go the distance with the rest of the gang promised outings on the earlier Walton show along with Vic.

'Make sure you are in Vic's corner on the night Harry, so we can all shout abuse at the television!' shouted Fatal as he welcomed him into the bar. 'Maybe the local newspaper will want to come here again for this story and more photos?'

Harry smiled and nodded to Big Gladys. 'Fatal has his eye on business again Gladys. If this keeps up you can ask him for a raise in wages.'

Fatal winced and Gladys feigned a shocked expression as Tommy reached the corner of the bar having heard what Harry had said. 'Go easy Harry or Fatal will start charging for admission to his television room!'

It was all good-natured banter and everyone seemed relaxed for a change. It had been a tough period following Brett's death but at last it seemed the corner had been turned.

§

Kenny's title defence was top of the bill at the Roborough Ice Rink which doubled as a stadium and had a capacity for six thousand punters. Jack Silver via Teddy and Sid offered Harry work for three of his fighters in six rounders so with Vic topping the undercard it looked a good night for the gym.

In the meantime everyone was training with a renewed enthusiasm and all appeared excited at the prospect of Vic's title fight and the earlier outing for him in an eight rounder with Chalky, Sam and now Jake making up the bill. Only Dicky and Johnny were without work on the two shows but Harry arranged for them to do the corner with Tommy both nights so they had a few quid to come in. Vic's opponent for the Walton show was a tough coloured kid who was known as a banger but he just nodded when Tommy told him who he had got, he never mentioned his forthcoming area title fight with Eddie Soames.

Harry always became suspicious when everything was going along without a problem. He didn't understand life enough to accept the good times for what they were, and he certainly did not trust success; always preparing for the moment when it would all go wrong. He believed things were never as they seemed to be.

Tommy lived for the day, moaning and cursing, rarely recognising good points in anyone - or if he did they were never acknowledged. This was his way of life; he lived for boxing, boozing and an ambition to get another champion. Tommy always claimed that nobody ever says those two words *Thank You*. In the world of boxing those two words do not exist.

Drinking to Tommy was life itself and Fatal's pub was an extension of the gym: a place to talk boxing and get drunk, both of which occurred with alarming regularity. He didn't care about much else; he defended his boxers at all times with the threat of violence, and yet the next minute he rained abuse upon them.

10

Harry drove his van onto the car park behind Walton's town hall, dodging piles of rubble where adjacent buildings had been demolished. The show was a joint Teddy and Sid promotion and a sure sell out with Vic's bout topping the bill and his stable supplying three other fighters. If this business keeps up, he thought, I should be able to get another taxi and perhaps a better van for taking the boys around. The insurance company were disputing the validity of Brett's driving licence and the legality of him driving a commercial vehicle in this country. As usual when confronted and questioned by apparent authority Harry had resorted to abuse, and frightened the insurance investigator, causing him to fall down the rickety stairs during his hurried escape from the gym. Needless to say this had slowed down any chance of an early settlement, if one was to be offered at all.

A smiling Sid met them all as they entered the rather ornate room where the weigh in was taking place. 'Great to see you and the boys Harry, Teddy will be along later and I hear even Jack Silver may attend just to say hello to everyone before the big title fight show.'

Harry was unusually relaxed as Chalky, Sam and Jake jumped on the scales in succession with nods of approval from the Board inspector and opposing boxer managers.

'The boys look in good shape Harry, and here's Vic and his opponent.'

The coloured kid, Bonny Webb weighed in first and was spot on the middleweight limit, while Vic was two pounds inside. They shook hands with a beaming Sid between them, posing for the camera and that was it. There was the usual cross talk and a few comments about the meteoric rise of Jack Silver in the boxing business and the syndicate that now seemed to control television but nothing nasty as all present knew it meant plenty of work.

'Now Tom, it's the usual routine,' said a chirpy Harry. 'Sid's got two rooms reserved for you and the boys and a snack laid on. I need to chat to him about the undercard on the title fight show and whether Vic will go on before the interval or just before Kenny. Both fights are being televised. . . I can then sort out Micky, Tony and Chris. Is everything alright, Tom, you seem very quiet?'

Tommy had that puzzled expression on his face again. He'd been sitting some distance from the weigh in looking intently at Vic.

'Yeah, fine but I still can't fathom out what's going on in Vic's head. This is his most important fight and the kid he's got is no phoney; he's a banger. The Board will be watching closely after agreeing to his Area Title fight yet Vic hasn't said a word about anything; not about this kid tonight; or Eddie Soames. He just goes on his own way. . . he's a fucking mystery.'

'Well that's how he is,' replied Harry. 'Don't try to fathom him out. . . best get to the hotel and some food and rest. Dicky and Johnny will be along later so you have plenty of help with the boys and the corner. I'll see you at the hotel.'

Tom stretched and yawned and seemed to relax a bit. 'Okay, all will be well. See you later.'

§

The van engine spluttered into life as the boys all piled in the back, laughing and joking. It was a tight squeeze with Dicky and Johnny getting a lift back having earlier hitched a ride on the way to the venue. Tommy sat in the passenger seat next to Harry and immediately started his normal post-fight tirade.

'Did you see that fucking Arthur Wells ringside with that young bird on his arm and him fucking eighty if he's a day. He brags about fighting in three world wars and there's not a scratch on him; I'll bet the little bastard has never even had a tooth ache. Made a fucking fortune from demolition, crooking everybody including the government and now tells people he's *got* religion - just trying to catch the ref 's eye now he's in his last fucking round. If there's two places to go his fucking card is marked for a trip down below. . . and,' he gasped, 'all his fucking money will go to that no-necked, chinless, ugly fucking midget son of his who was hob nobbing all night long with the posers, including that great fat, blond-haired slut who was married to Jeffy Wall - him who was found dead in his swimming pool. What a fucking outfit!'

It just wouldn't be the same if Tommy failed to deliver his usual torrent of abuse about all and sundry after a boxing show. It was greeted with howls of laughter and Harry turned his head in an effort to hide a broad grin as Chalky's reply, in his up market English accent, sent them all rolling about.

'And that gentlemen is Mr Thomas Law's appraisal of the ringside clientele who attended the boxing show tonight.'

Tommy was grinning as he sank down in the passenger seat feigning sleep. It had been a successful evening's work, Chalky and Sam winning and Jake on his feet at the end. Vic did the business and now all was set for his title fight.'

Before his fight Vic was told to be careful as his opponent had a knockout punch with his right hand, and to watch out for his head as a cut would ruin his chances of the title fight. He did nothing for the first two rounds and got caught with the big right hook towards the end of the third that every one in the hall saw coming. But Vic took it squarely on the chin, shrugged his shoulders and hardly took a step back. The next round he cut loose with a vicious attack and Webb sank to the canvas. He was up at eight but in no state to continue and the referee called it off.

Back in the dressing room Tom had asked him what he was trying to do early on and he replied he was waiting for Webb to do something and if that right hand was the best he had then he might as well finish him.

§

'Are you lot okay in the back, and no problems with you Vic?' shouted Harry, as the van trundled along.

'All's well back here boss. . . Vic's asleep,' answered Chalky, as they all settled down as best they could.

All round it had been a good night.

11

Although 'burst' is perhaps not quite the right word to describe Coupon's entry into the Cricketers Arms at mid-day it was certainly with a turn of speed he had lacked in recent years.

'Albert I have great news for you,' he shouted, visibly excited. 'I visited the council office this morning to get some information about the work they intend doing around here and it's all coming down over the next few years, except your pub. Because it's a Victorian building they are going to preserve it and then build houses all around! How about that?'

Fatal sat slumped on a stool behind the bar and raised his head with some difficulty.

'I don't personally need any fucking preserving after the booze I had last night with Harry and the gang; but good news Coup, let's hope they keep their word.'

'It's all down on plans for you to see, it's a wonder they haven't written to you about it!' chortled a delighted Coupon.

Just then Doríce swept in after no doubt listening to the conversation from behind the door.

'Good morning Stanley and yes, I *was* aware of the proposed plans but decided not to burden Albert with extra mental stress. I am informed that our efforts to promote this business and the pub's historical importance helped them to reach their decision but after that deplorable spectacle here last night with Eric I fear for the future.'

'Now look here Doríce,' mumbled Fatal, as he attempted to straighten up but the effort was too much for him. 'Eric kept larking about with Micky and the boys but I know they shouldn't have given him that glass of mixed drinks. He went down like a sack of spuds and round and round he went like a top. What a sight. . . you saw him Coup!'

Coupon turned away and smiled, remembering the sight of Eric spinning around on the floor like a Catherine Wheel with people trying to grab him as he went by.

'Anyway Doríce,' Coupon said, reverting at once to his usual hang-dog facial expression. 'It's not the first time Eric's had a turn. Harry put him in his taxi with the help of the boxers and off he went to hospital with Gladys restraining him. All's well now as I saw him earlier walking about as if nothing had happened. . . but great news about the pub's future: I'll bet the local Press will like the story.'

'Yes Stanley, I shall be contacting the newspaper editor whom I know on a personal basis and arrange an interview here on the premises. Hopefully when Eric is under control and that lot from upstairs are absent.'

'Well Doríce. . .' interrupted Fatal, 'that *lot from upstairs* keep this place going day after day and now they're on television everything looks good. I can't get rid of Eric as I told his aunty, who turned out to be his mother, that I would always give him a job should anything happen to her and now she's down one of those holes I'm keeping my word.'

§

Doríce visibly shuddered whenever she looked at Fatal: it wasn't only his way of expressing himself but also his general appearance.

'Albert, Beatrice was a lady who unfortunately fell under the spell of a gay young army officer early in the war and Eric was the result. He should not touch alcohol at all as it disagrees with his medication; if he died on the premises I really don't know how I would face my committee members. Please pay more attention to what's going on behind the bar and less time encouraging the riff raff in the corner.'

'Alright, I'll do my best with Eric but I think Coup wants another payment off the television,' grunted out an exhausted Fatal. 'It will be standing room only in here for Vic's fight.'

Coupon looked up when his name was mentioned. He'd heard all the squabbling many times before.

'I trust you're pleased with your new acquisition Doríce. It does show acute business acumen on your part,' he said in a grovelling tone of voice. 'Ten pounds should do for now.'

'Of course Stanley, right away,' replied a now beaming Doríce as she headed triumphantly out of the bar. 'I will leave you to handle it, Albert. Put the receipt in the till.'

'Thank you Doríce,' shouted Coupon. He fumbled in the pocket of his shabby overcoat. 'Oh, and Albert, I have a few tickets left for Vic's fight at the right price so tell the usual jibbers to get their money out!'

§

It was good to see all the boxers in the gym early evening. With plenty of work and Vic's area title fight arranged, a new spirit had drifted into their training. Tommy was back to form, abusing them again and everybody else he could think of and Harry was good for a sub against their next payday. So when a scuffling and thudding came from the stairs coupled with gasping for breath it made Harry leave his desk to investigate. There was Fatal halfway up the stairs.

'Harry,' he blurted out gasping, 'you must ring Teddy Long right away. . . he's been trying to contact you; something very urgent.'

With that supreme effort out of the way he collapsed on the stairs with his head in his hands.

A broad smile crossed Harry's face as shouted into the gym. 'Tom, come here quick and help Fatal, he looks in a bad way. I've got to ring Teddy urgently and see what's up.'

Tommy appeared on the landing with Jake looking over his shoulder. 'Let's get him back down into the pub Jake,' muttered Tommy, trying not to laugh out loud. 'What a fucking state he's in!'

§

'Is that you Teddy, I've a message to ring you!'

Teddy's voice was strangely quiet but his message hit Harry like a bombshell. 'Kenny's opponent has been injured in training and can't make the title fight date. Jack's been going mad, television arranged, every ticket sold, loads of sponsors. He was with the Board all morning and they've come up with a solution, but it's up to you Harry.'

He paused for a moment as if fearful of what he was about to say and the silence un-nerved Harry.

'Well, what is it?' he asked.

'They're prepared to postpone Vic's area title fight and he can go in with Kenny for a ten round non-title bout. This will save the show and keep everyone happy. What do you say Harry?'

Harry lent heavily on his desk, hardly able to take in what Teddy had said and stammered. 'I'll ring you back after speaking to Tom.'

'Right Harry but it will have to be today as we must know. The fight's only two weeks away and there's the press to take care of. Money is no object here, and we will owe you if you can do it. Jack's by the telephone now waiting for my call. . . I know you'll do your best.'

Harry put back the phone and sat down, strange thoughts racing through his head. What was he to do? How could he okay the bout? Kenny was vastly experienced and a good fighter, but how good was Vic? Anyway Tom would veto the fight as he didn't trust Jack Silver and was suspicious of anybody in boxing who was in a more prominent or influential position than he was. Yes! That would be the answer: let Tom kill the deal. He would thank Teddy and Jack for considering Vic but at this stage of his career an area title fight was his ceiling.

He let out a deep sigh of relief believing the problem could be quickly resolved and the decision taken out of his hands.

'Tom! I need you right away, quick as you can. Something's come up and we need to talk.'

Tommy stopped showing Chalky a slick move, hurried into the office and laughingly shouted. 'What's up that can be all so earth shattering? Has Fatal dropped fucking dead, or has Coupon bought a round of drinks?'

'Best sit down Tom and listen to this,' said Harry, managing a weak smile. 'Norton is injured and has pulled out of the fight. Jack Silver's been with the Board all day and they've agreed to a ten round non-title fight if Vic can step in and if all parties agree. . .'

He got no further as Tommy interrupted, 'We'll take the fight. Tell the bastards it's on!'

'Harry jumped up out of his chair and spread his arms wide in disbelief. 'Hold on Tom, hold on a minute. Vic is a good prospect but that's all after a few fights. Kenny may not be a great champion but he got there on merit and has loads of experience. He will be after Vic from the bell. Let's talk this thing over.'

Tom walked up to the desk as Harry sat down again. 'Take this fight Harry or I'm down those fucking stairs for the last time. You owe it to me after what happened to Billy!'

Harry shuddered and was speechless. He'd completely misjudged Tom's reaction to the news and his outburst and reference to Billy shocked him. Is that how he'd felt all along and deep down held him responsible for his death?

His thoughts were interrupted by a gathering of the boxers, crowding into the office doorway. 'And what the fuck do you lot want?' he bellowed at them. 'This is not your business; get back training.'

It was Micky who answered in a strangely cold and calculated voice. 'We couldn't help hearing the conversation Harry. It *is* our business: Billy was one of us; we grew up with him from the beginning right through to the end. You don't just owe Tommy; you owe all of us, and Vic deserves his chance.'

Harry could not believe Micky had said that, and was shocked at the venom in his voice. He slumped back in his chair and an eerie silence fell on the room. 'You fucking lot are out of your minds but if that's the way you all feel I'll go along with it. Now get the fuck out of my office while I ring Teddy.'

The cheer that went up from the doorway un-nerved Harry. 'Okay Tom,' he spluttered. 'We don't want a row after all these years together. At the end of the day Vic is your fighter so get on with it.'

Tom nodded, grinned, punched the air and headed back into the gym.

§

Vic's fight with the champion was soon the talk of the town and the pub became the focal point for every boxing follower and loony who thought he knew what was going on. The atmosphere was just like when Billy Stone got his title shot although in Vic's case anything less than a good showing would put him right out of the picture. He didn't seem to change his training or general demeanour, still having a few drinks with the boys then going off home with Rita. He spoke only to the other boxers unless cornered, but gave a good interview to the local paper in which he praised Kenny Cole as a fine champion, while complimenting Harry and Tommy for everything they'd done for him. Even Fatal and Dorice got a mention for their 'untiring support' of the boxers. It made good reading.

Harry explained to everyone that Kenny's title was not at stake and even if Vic won he would not be champion. Vic was a substitute for the *bona fide* challenger and anyway his record did not merit him fighting for the title at this stage of his career. But a good display would shoot him up the ratings and there could be a title fight for him in the future.

After a few days had passed Harry called Vic into the office for a chat as he had shown little emotion and made no comment during the heated exchange of words with Tommy and the boxers when the bout with Kenny was argued over; just nodding his head when an agreement was reached to take the fight.

'You need to be at your best against Kenny,' Harry muttered. 'No flashy stuff, and watch out for his head when he comes in close. Don't think about anything else but survival. Your job is to be there at the end and that for you will be a great result. Remember, I'm your manager and what success you might get in the ring depends as much on what happens out of it. I don't like this fight but get on with it and make a name for your self. I'll get back to you in a day or so about your wages, it will be a good payday for you. Now is there anything you want to ask me?'

Vic shook his head in that strange way of his and replied. 'No Harry, all's well. I saw Kenny in his title defence and no problems there for me.'

Harry straightened up and looked Vic squarely in the face. 'You be careful. He'll be after you from round one and a stoppage win for him will be expected.'

A smile flickered across Vic's face as he walked slowly towards the door; then stopping he looked back at Harry who was leaning his elbows on the desk, head in his hands. Raising his voice he half shouted. 'Thanks Harry for giving me my chance. I won't let you down!'

§

The national sporting press picked up the story and somehow Vic's background became news: someone, somewhere had given them details of his early days as a foundling followed by orphanages and the army. They played the fight up as a 'rags to riches' chance for him and the story caught the public's imagination and certainly gave him celebrity status.

Everyone tried to keep the newspaper stories from him but it was impossible and a drunken Fatal didn't help by chatting to a stranger when no one else was around, defending himself later by saying he didn't know the bloke was a reporter.

The only person who failed to comment on it all was Vic and when Rita questioned him on how he felt about it all he just shrugged his shoulders and said. 'Well it's the truth.'

Harry spent most of the time at Vonnie's house boring her with doubts over his decision to take the fight and wishing he had been firmer with the lot of them. His visits to the pub got fewer as fight night approached and he arranged for Tommy to take the boxers to the weigh in as Micky, Tony and Chris were also on the bill with Dicky and Johnny helping in the corner again. He made the excuse he had to attend to some legal business and would be there in the evening. Tommy made no comment and knew that things were not as they should be but carried on like the true professional he was.

§

Nobody knew Kenny Cole better that Tommy Law. He had taken on a mediocre amateur middleweight boxer and turned him into a future British Champion. Never as skilful or charismatic as Billy Stone and always boxing under his shadow Kenny nevertheless developed into a good fighter. His aggressive front foot style and constant attack tended to wear down opponents. Not being a one punch knockout fighter it was the cumulative effect of Kenny's punches that won him bouts. He had a few blotches on his record but had reversed each of those defeats. Hour after hour Tommy had shown Vic how to counteract the two handed attacks which would be non stop and to wait for openings - that would come - to deliver his solid punches. Tommy had even cut back on his boozing and stopped abusing everyone, but they all knew that wouldn't last!

With an extravagant lifestyle and spending more than he earned, Kenny had left the gym owing a few quid to his fellow boxers; money they could ill afford to lose. So perhaps there was a score to settle and it was Vic they all had in mind to carry that out. Harry had commented to Tommy on one of his rare visits to the gym that everyone seemed intent on helping Vic to prepare for the fight, lining up to spar him as they all knew Kenny's style and followed Tommy's instructions to the letter. Vic did all that was asked of him and only showed annoyance when he was told by Tom to cut out any sex play on the run up to the fight as this had been said with a certain amount of venom in earshot of the rest of the boxers. He soon recovered and realised how important this bout was, not only to him but to the rest of his gym mates, the management, and all his supporters.

§

Harry called in to the pub one morning a few days before the big fight, after clearing up things in the office when the gym was empty and there were no distractions. Vic's training was going along fine and Tom reported back to him most days and kept him in the picture on everything.

Fatal was behind a deserted bar bottling up after the previous night's business.

'Morning Harry, you're up and about early. . . another great night's business; the place was packed, everyone talking about the fight. All the tickets have gone and Coupon bought some drinks: that shows how serious things are!'

Harry smiled at Fatal. For all his faults he put up with a lot from his customers. 'I've just checked everything out for the big night and all seems well. No problems down here I need to know about?'

'No Harry. The boys have been taking it steady lately. All Vic has is an orange squash. Tommy's still going strong but everybody's in a great mood and looking forward to the fight.'

'Okay then Albert I'll be off. Keep up the good work!'

He'd almost reached the door when Fatal shouted. 'Oh Harry, I almost forgot to tell you, a lady came in here earlier. I'd left the front door open for some fresh air to swish about and before I knew it she was standing at the bar looking at Billy's photo. She said she would like to speak to Victor Lane. I explained he wasn't here but could I take a message for him, but she said no and would try to call again. She was a smart women Harry. . . not an old scrubber.'

Harry felt a cold shiver run up his back. 'Did you ask her what she wanted Vic for?' he asked moving closer to Fatal at the bar.

'Well no Harry, I didn't really have a chance. When I said he wasn't here she left.'

100

Suddenly Harry felt angry with Fatal for not getting more information; such as her name and the reason why she called.

He knew he could always expect people to come out of the woodwork when stories like Vic's appeared in the daily newspapers, but he must play this down with only a few days to go to the big fight.

'Now listen Albert, keep this lady and her visit to yourself. No mention to Vic, Doríce or Rita; and for fuck's sake not to Tommy. Nobody must know. Now *do* you understand me?'

'Yes Harry, yes. Not a word from me to anybody. . . you can rely on me, you know that.'

'Thanks, I must be off now. I know I can trust you.'

He walked slowly out through the bar door and into the street. Surely no upsets when all seemed to be going so well, but this was boxing. Take nothing for granted.

§

The day of reckoning had arrived and Harry knew he should go to the fight but realised that he would never make it. Earlier that morning he'd received a message from Tommy via Willie his taxi driver that everyone was ready, in order and on time, and they were leaving for the venue and noon weigh in.

He hadn't left his rooms all day preferring to be alone with his thoughts.

He poured himself another large scotch, looked around his dingy flat, and up at the loudly ticking clock on the wall. Things could all have been so different. Well. . . almost ten o'clock and the main event would be over by now. Time to face everybody. He downed the last drop with a heavy sigh, locked his flat door and went out into the dimly lit street. The pub was only a few hundred yards away but he dragged his feet as if anywhere was better then where he must go.

Slowly approaching the old building, smoke had escaped through the bar windows forming a moving white shroud like ghosts waiting to greet him. The noise increased as he got nearer: a babble of voices, each one getting higher in an effort to make themselves heard. He opened the bar door and took a step back. It was packed solid with every face in the district, all grinning, laughing and shouting at no one in particular.

'Here he comes! The champion maker!' hooted Coupon. Suddenly Harry was conscious of Doríce in his face, planting a kiss on his cheek; Erwin behind her. 'Congratulations Mr Keys! Fantastic!'

Harry couldn't move either way with the crowd surging around him, all slapping him on the back. Rita was behind the bar, dabbing her eyes, Big Gladys with her arm around her.

'You're a crafty one Harry,' Doríce purred in his ear. 'But then I always knew that.'

He pushed his way through the crowd to the bar, feeling confused and aggressive. Fatal stood with a bottle of whisky in one hand and a tumbler in the other. 'Your money is no good tonight Harry!' he exclaimed with a huge grin. Eric was smiling over his shoulder.

'For fuck's sake Fatal, what's all this about?' he shouted.

Fatal looked stunned. 'Didn't Tommy contact you? We even sent Eric round to your flat in case he couldn't, but he got lost. Vic knocked Kenny out in the fifth round; was all over him. We thought you must have heard. It was all on TV; you should have seen Teddy Long's face at the end - a fucking picture of misery.'

For Harry everything suddenly seemed to go quiet, just a slight buzzing in his ears. All the faces were detached like comic strips: Fatal's mouth was moving, Eric was still smiling and Doríce was still by his side. What has happened? he thought. What has fucking happened?

The noise returned with such force that Harry felt suddenly giddy, maybe the scotch or the bedlam in the bar; everyone turned to the door and a deafening roar erupted that brought the hairs up on his neck. It was Tommy, his fist raised in triumphal salute; Vic just behind him with that quizzical look on his face as if he was puzzled that anyone could have imagined the fight was going to turn out any other way. The other boxers followed, all grinning and punching the air. The crowd descended on them.

Finally Tommy caught Harry's gaze and gave him a broad grin and a nod - all that was needed and said everything. Harry lifted his glass and took a long drink as Fatal's voice penetrated the hubbub.

'Here we go again Harry, just like old times. Vic's bound to get a title fight after tonight isn't he?'

Harry swallowed the whisky and put his glass down. He felt so tired and rubbed his eyes. . . yes, there was the hint of a tear there. Fatal refilled his glass, Harry raised it up high, and another stupendous cheer erupted.

'You're right Albert; you are right: a title shot,' he sighed, leaning heavily on the bar. 'Off we go again. . . but always remember, at the end of the day nothing is ever as it seems to be.'

WANTED

DEAD OR ALIVE

Bill Longley

DESCRIPTION

He is about six feet tall, weight 150 pounds, tolerably spare built, black hair, eyes and whiskers, slightly stooped in the shoulders. Those who know him say that he can be recognized in a crowd of 100 by the keeness and blackness of his eyes.

1000,00 DOLLARS Reward!

'I may be a killer, I may be a murderer, but I never stole a horse.' -

Wild Bill Longley

Wild Bill Longley - Texas Gunslinger by Dick Brownson.
192 pages. 25 Illustrations. £9.99 from all good bookshops.
'I may be a killer; I may be a murderer; but I never stole a horse,' Bill Longley.
'Beautifully written and intensely readable. . .' Review www.amazon.co.uk

Edward Gaskell
publishers
DEVON

Lazarus Press
DEVON